CW01659229

The Absolute Beginner's Guide to Using AI

How to Use AI to Save Time, Work Smarter, and Get More Done - Without Feeling Overwhelmed

Alastair McDermott

Authority Press

Copyright © 2025 by Alastair McDermott. All rights reserved.

No part of this book may be reproduced in any form or by any electronic or mechanical means, including information storage and retrieval systems, without written permission from the author, except for the use of brief quotations in a book review.

AI Usage Policy

> To state it unequivocally: I'm Alastair, a human being, and the author of this book. I use AI tools extensively – as you'll see in this book! – but I will never use them to produce low-quality, automated rubbish. That is my promise to you.

ISBN 9798341149748 (Paperback)
ISBN 9798286262441 (Hardcover)
ISBN (Ebook coming soon)
ISBN (Audiobook coming soon)

Published by Authority Press · AuthorityPress.EU · Sales@AuthorityPress.EU

Second Edition (v2.0) Last Updated: 4th June 2025

The information in this book is provided "as is," without any guarantees or warranties, expressed or implied. The publisher and author are not responsible for any damages resulting from the use of the information in this book, including direct, indirect, incidental, punitive, and consequential damages.

Trademarks: All brand and product names used in this book are trademarks of their respective owners. Their use does not imply any affiliation or endorsement by the trademark owners.

Contents

Resources

Looking for Practical Tools and Templates?

To help you apply the strategies from *The Absolute Beginner's Guide to Using AI*, I've created a set of free companion resources - including checklists, prompt templates, and quick-start guides - all designed to make your AI journey easier and more effective.

You can download them anytime at **humanspark.ai/resources**.

Whether you're looking to streamline your workflow, improve your prompting skills, or build your personal AI system, these tools will give you a head start - no technical background required.

Author's Note

If you're reading this book in 2025, I've just updated this book to the 2nd Edition to keep up with the newest AI tools, versions, and updates. If you bought an electronic version of the book directly from me at my website I'll be emailing you an updated copy of the book whenever I update.

You can also check for new versions with me directly at alastair@humanspark.ai – I read and reply to all emails personally and love to get feedback and suggestions.

Introduction

AI is here. Are you ready?

Like many, I grew up watching Star Trek where intelligent computers and talking robots were centuries away. It was fun, but firmly in the realm of make-believe. Yet, here we are.

We might not be travelling at 'Warp 9' just yet, but we do have intelligent computers we can talk to, and even tools that can understand and act on what we ask. Imagine needing a quick draft for a client email, or wanting to brainstorm 10 new ideas for a blog post - and having a tool deliver that in seconds, without you breaking a sweat (and this is just the tip of the iceberg in terms of what they can do).

The world is changing quickly. AI is here. It is changing jobs and industries, and it is reshaping how we work. You have likely seen the headlines, heard the buzz, and perhaps even tried a few AI tools yourself. But you might also feel a bit overwhelmed. You might be uncertain about how to make sense of this fast-moving landscape and how to use AI in a way that truly helps you.

You might fear you are not tech-savvy enough, or that it will take too much time to learn. That is exactly why I wrote this book. This book is for you - the working professional who wants to use AI to get more done, save time, and stay competitive, without needing to become a tech expert.

You might be thinking, 'I am not a tech person. Do I really need AI?' The answer is a clear 'yes'. AI is not just for software developers or big corporations; it is a powerful assistant for anyone who wants to work smarter, not harder. Imagine saving hours on repetitive tasks, freeing up your time for strategy, creativity, or even more personal time. Think about growing your business by producing content faster, or staying competitive by understanding new market insights. AI helps you do all of this.

This is important because in today's fast-changing professional world, staying relevant and efficient is key to your success. You do not need to understand complex algorithms or learn to code - this book will show you how to use AI tools, step by step, in plain English, to achieve your goals.

To truly grasp this, think of AI as your new, incredibly efficient personal assistant. This assistant works tirelessly, is always available, and can handle a surprising amount of work - as long as you give clear instructions. It is not here to replace you, but to help you.

Just like a good human assistant, your AI helper can take on the tasks that drain your time and energy, allowing you to focus on the parts of your work that truly matter and where your unique skills shine. Throughout this book, we will often refer to AI in this way - as a helpful, powerful tool at your service, enhancing your professional output and making a greater impact through your work.

So, what exactly will this book do for you? This book is a practical guide for professionals at every level - whether you're an employee, manager, entrepreneur, or business owner - for anyone who wants to share their knowledge and insights more effectively, and use AI to make a meaningful difference in the world. It is a culmination of my own experience in helping professionals and organisations use technology, packed with practical insights.

Specifically, in this book, you will discover how to:

- **Expand Your Reach:** Use AI to connect with more people, gain insights from data, and create engaging content that helps you share your expertise.
- **Increase Your Efficiency:** Automate repetitive tasks, organise your workflow, and save time so you can focus on important activities like strategy, creativity, and building relationships.
- **Use AI Wisely and Safely:** Create a plan for using AI responsibly, protect data privacy, reduce bias, and build trust.
- **Stay Relevant:** Learn the skills and strategies to keep up with the changing AI landscape, ensuring your expertise stays important and useful for years to come.

What this book will *not* do is turn you into a computer programmer or a deep AI researcher. We will not explore complex mathematical models or dive into the intricacies of neural networks. The goal is not to make you an AI scientist, but to make you a confident, effective user of AI tools in your daily work.

Now, let's look at your AI journey. This book is designed to guide you step-by-step, building your confidence with every chapter. We start with the basics, ensuring you get some early wins that show you just how simple and powerful AI can be. This book will guide you from the very basics of what AI is and how to get started, through practical applications like using chatbots and mastering prompts, all the way to understanding ethical considerations and integrating AI into your daily workflow. You'll gain the skills to confidently use AI tools to boost your productivity, expand your reach, and ultimately, transform how you work.

AI is here. Are you ready? You are.

The journey to becoming an AI-powered professional does not require a technical degree or endless hours of complex study. It does require curiosity and a willingness to learn. This book provides that first step, and every step after. You have everything you need to begin transforming your work with AI. Let us start building the foundation that will keep you adaptable as AI continues to evolve.

Chapter 1

What is AI?

And Why Should You Care?

AI is software that performs tasks requiring human intelligence - like learning, problem-solving, and decision-making.

If you're like most business owners I talk to, you've heard the hype but aren't sure what's real. You might worry about privacy, wonder if it's worth your time, or fear it'll replace your work.

This chapter cuts through the noise. I'll show you exactly how AI works, what it does well, and how to use it responsibly. More importantly, you'll see practical ways it can save you hours each week on repetitive tasks - freeing you to focus on the work only you can do.

AI's core function is pattern recognition on a vast scale. Just as humans learn from examples, AI processes immense datasets to identify trends, relationships, and anomalies, enabling it to perform specific jobs like generating text, recognising images, or predicting market behaviour.

For example, you could open an AI tool like ChatGPT and type: Suggest three blog post ideas about [your industry topic]. This gives you an instant start.

You're probably using AI every day without even realising it. It runs quietly in the background of many services we use:

- Netflix uses AI to suggest films and TV shows you might enjoy based on what you've watched before.
- Your email service uses it to filter out spam messages, keeping your inbox cleaner.
- When you unlock your phone with your face, that's AI at work.

Beyond these common examples, think about the customer service chatbots you find on websites - they're powered by AI to answer your questions quickly. The personalised adverts that pop up in your social media feeds also use AI to show you things you might be interested in. Even the predictive text that helps you type faster on your phone uses AI to guess your next word.

Tools like Siri or Google Assistant, and grammar checkers like Grammarly, also rely on AI to make our digital interactions smoother and more efficient.

AI isn't just for entertainment or making things convenient. It can help with everyday tasks too. Imagine using AI to find recipes based on the ingredients you already have in your fridge, or to create a shopping list for your weekly meals. You could tell an AI recipe generator what's in your cupboard, and it could instantly suggest meal ideas, complete with instructions and even nutritional information. This saves you time and reduces food waste.

AI is also helping to solve big problems in many different areas. In healthcare, it helps doctors diagnose diseases earlier and plan more effective treatments. In schools, AI creates learning tools that adapt to each student's pace and style, making education more personal. In transport, AI is a key part of developing self-driving cars, which aim to make roads safer and reduce traffic jams.

AI is changing how we work. It can handle boring, repetitive tasks like data entry, scheduling appointments, or answering simple customer questions. This frees us up to do more interesting, creative, and strategic work. AI can also spot patterns in huge amounts of data - far more than a human could process - helping businesses make better, more informed decisions.

Consider Alex, a freelance graphic designer who used to spend hours manually categorising client feedback from various sources. By implementing a simple AI tool, she now feeds all comments into it, and the AI summarises key themes and actionable tasks in minutes. This frees her to focus on design work, taking on more projects and delivering faster.

Or John, a solo marketing consultant, who uses AI to brainstorm social media campaign ideas and draft initial ad copy, cutting his content creation time by half.
For independent consultants, coaches, freelancers, and solopreneurs like you, AI offers a powerful way to improve your work. Imagine AI helping you with:

- **Content Creation:** AI can help you generate outlines for blog posts, draft social media captions, write email newsletters, or even take your long articles and turn them into shorter, engaging snippets for different platforms. This means you can produce more high-quality content consistently.
- **Research:** Instead of spending hours sifting through countless articles, AI can quickly summarise key insights from reports or research papers. It can even help you find specific data points, saving you valuable time that you can then use for client work or business development.

- **Client Management:** AI can help you draft initial client communications, organise meeting notes, or even suggest follow-up actions based on conversation transcripts. This streamlines your client interactions and ensures you don't miss important details.

- **Marketing:** From generating creative ideas for ad copy to analysing website traffic patterns for better targeting, AI can make your marketing efforts more efficient. It helps you reach your ideal audience more effectively, without needing a large marketing team.

- **Idea Generation:** Feeling stuck? AI can be a fantastic brainstorming partner. You can feed it a problem or a topic, and it can generate a wide range of ideas, helping you break through creative blocks and find new angles for your work.

- **Learning & Development:** AI can help you quickly learn new skills or understand complex topics by summarising information, explaining concepts, or even acting as a tutor. This means you can stay sharp and adapt to new trends faster.

Why does this matter to you? AI represents a significant shift in how we use technology, and it's here to stay. Understanding and using AI can make you much more efficient in your work, studies, and daily life. The key benefit is that it helps you achieve more of what you want - serving more clients, creating more impact, or simply having more free time. In a world where everyone is trying to stand out, AI offers a unique advantage. It's not about letting AI do all the work for you. Instead, it's about using it as a "force multiplier" - a tool that amplifies your unique insights, expertise, and creativity. This allows you to produce more high-quality content, reach a wider audience, and strengthen your position as an authority in your field, all without burning yourself out.

AI also brings up important questions. We need to think about privacy, job impacts, and fairness. We'll examine these in more detail later in the book. This matters because as AI becomes a bigger part of our lives, we need to use it responsibly. While AI offers incredible opportunities, it also raises critical considerations: how do we ensure our personal and client data remains private when we use AI tools? How will AI change the future of work for independent professionals, and how can we adapt? And how do we make sure AI systems are fair and don't show bias? We'll explore these critical points in detail later in the book, because using AI effectively goes hand-in-hand with using it responsibly.

Learning about AI now isn't just about keeping up. It's about preparing for what's next. As AI continues to grow and develop, people who know how to work with it will have a clear advantage. AI can help you reach your goals and explore new possibilities in your business and personal life.

Key Takeaways

- AI mimics human thinking to perform tasks, acting as a smart assistant.
- You likely use AI daily in many common services and apps.
- AI can significantly boost productivity for independent professionals.
- It automates repetitive tasks and enhances creative

work.

- Understanding AI is crucial for staying competitive and expanding your influence.
- Responsible AI use involves considering privacy, job impacts, and fairness.

Next Steps

Consider this: Identify three tasks you do often that are repetitive or time-consuming - whether for work, home, or personal activities. Write them down. Now, for each task, ask yourself: *How specifically could AI assist with this?* For example, could a chatbot draft an email faster? Could an AI summariser help you digest research more quickly? Or perhaps an AI content generator could help you brainstorm ideas for a new workshop? Jot down your initial thoughts on the potential AI solution for each. We'll look at these tasks again later and see how AI might make them easier.

AI isn't a scary robot that's going to take over. How we use AI is up to us. We choose how it's made and what it's for. By learning about AI, you're taking the first step to using it to improve your life and work. Let's explore this together!

Chapter 2

AI Tools

How to Access Them

You can start using AI right now. No coding required. No technical background needed. This chapter shows you the two main ways to access AI: through websites and smartphone apps. We'll cover which tools to trust, how to spot official versions, and what you need to know about privacy.

The AI landscape changes fast, with new tools appearing weekly. I'll help you navigate this without getting overwhelmed.

When we refer to "AI tools," we typically mean online services or applications that use Artificial Intelligence to complete specific tasks. Consider them smart assistants designed to make your work simpler and quicker. These are not complex software requiring installation or coding. Instead, they are ready-to-use solutions accessible with a few clicks or taps.

Accessing AI Tools Online

Many AI tools are available as websites. This is often the simplest way to begin, as you can use them on any device with an internet connection and a web browser - whether that is your laptop, desktop computer, or a tablet. Online tools offer significant advantages:

- **No Installation Needed:** They don't take up any

storage space on your device.

- **Always Up-to-Date:** The companies behind these tools handle all the updates, so you're always using the latest version with the newest features and improvements.
- **Accessibility:** You can access them from anywhere, as long as you have an internet connection.

Here are some popular AI tool websites you can try:

- **ChatGPT.com:** This is a powerful AI chatbot from OpenAI, excellent for writing, brainstorming, summarising information, and problem-solving. It is widely used and serves as an effective starting point.
- **Claude.ai:** Another capable AI chatbot from Anthropic, recognised for its ability to manage longer conversations and its analytical skills. Many find it particularly effective for detailed text analysis and creative writing.
- **Gemini.google.com:** Google's AI chatbot, which often integrates well with other Google services you may already use, such as Gmail or Google Docs.
- **Canva.com:** While primarily a design tool, Canva includes AI features that can help you create graphics, presentations, and social media content more quickly. For example, its "Magic Design" can generate designs from a text prompt.
- **Otter.ai:** This AI tool specialises in transcribing speech to text in real-time. It is very useful for recording meetings, interviews, or lectures and obtaining an accurate written record.

Many of these platforms offer free accounts. These free versions are usually sufficient to get you started and to explore their basic capabilities. However, they might have limits on how much you can use them or restrict access to certain advanced features. Always check the terms of service or pricing pages to understand what you are getting with a free account and if there are any usage caps.

AI Apps: On the Go

Most major AI tools also offer dedicated smartphone applications. These apps make it very convenient to use AI on your phone or tablet, allowing you to integrate AI into your daily routine, even when you are away from your computer. You can download these apps from your device's app store (such as the Apple App Store for iPhones or Google Play Store for Android devices).

Apps are particularly useful for tasks you perform often or when you want to use features specific to your phone, such as:

- **Camera Integration:** Some AI apps can analyse images taken with your phone's camera.
- **Voice Dictation:** You can often speak directly to the AI, which is great for drafting notes or messages on the go.
- **Voice Mode Conversations:** Many chatbots now offer a voice mode, allowing you to have a natural conversation with the AI, almost like talking to a person. This can be very useful for brainstorming or getting quick answers while multitasking.

Download the Right App

When downloading apps, it is important to ensure you are getting the official version from the actual AI company. There are often many unofficial or copycat apps that might not be secure or have the same functionality as the official apps. To stay safe:

- **Look for "Official":** Check the app listing for words like "Official" or "By [Company Name]".
- **Verify the Developer:** Always confirm that the developer listed in the app store is the legitimate company that created the AI tool. For example, for **ChatGPT**, ensure the developer is "**OpenAI**," for **Claude** ensure the developer is "Anthropic", etc.
- **Read Reviews:** While not foolproof, checking recent reviews can sometimes flag issues with unofficial apps.

Taking these precautions helps keep your data safe and ensures you are using the real, reliable tool.

A Word on Privacy (and Why Free Isn't Always Free)

When you use AI tools – especially those that process text, voice, or images - you're often sharing information with the company behind the tool. That input may be stored, analyzed, or even used to train future versions of the AI. This makes **privacy awareness essential**, especially if you're handling anything sensitive, confidential, or client-related.

One important distinction to understand is that **free and paid versions of AI tools are not created equal** – not just in features, but in how your data is handled.

- **Free tools often retain and reuse your data** to improve their models. That means what you type might be stored and potentially reviewed.
- **Paid versions typically offer more robust privacy options** – including ways to opt out of data sharing or promises not to use your data for training at all. This is especially important for professionals, consultants, or anyone working with proprietary or personal information.

Before using any new AI tool - especially for business - take a few minutes to check the privacy policy. This document explains how your data is collected, stored, used, and protected. It's not always easy reading, but understanding it is critical for protecting yourself and your clients.

Tip: You can paste a privacy policy into an AI chatbot and ask it to summarise the key points about data usage. This saves time and helps you make informed decisions.

This chapter gives you the essentials, but we'll explore data privacy, ethical use, and AI risk management in more depth later on in the dedicated **AI-Powered Data Privacy Matrix™** chapter.

This initial exploration aims for familiarisation, not mastery. The goal is to see how simple it is to interact with these tools and gain a sense of their capabilities. You do not need to create accounts for everything yet, but feel free to try signing up for one and simply experiment and see what is possible. The more you interact, the more comfortable and confident you will become. We'll cover signing up with ChatGPT more in-depth in the next chapter if you need more help.

Your Quick Win: Experiment with One AI Tool

Now that you understand how to access AI tools, here is a quick way to gain practical experience:

1. **Visit ChatGPT.com or open its official app.** Spend 5-10 minutes exploring the interface. Try typing a simple question, such as "What is a good morning routine for a busy professional?" or "Give me three ideas for a social media post about saving time." Observe how quickly it responds.

2. **Explore one other AI tool from the lists above.** For example, if you perform a lot of design work, try Canva's AI features. If you record many meetings, examine Otter.ai. Focus on understanding its purpose and how it generates results.

Key Takeaways

- **Accessibility is Key:** AI tools are primarily accessible online through websites and dedicated smartphone apps, requiring no complex installation or technical expertise.

- **Online Benefits:** Web-based tools offer convenience, are always up-to-date, and free up your device's storage.

- **Mobile Convenience:** AI apps provide on-the-go access and use phone-specific features like camera integration and voice dictation.

- **Verify Official Sources:** Always download apps from official developers to ensure security and reliability.

- **Understand Privacy:** Be aware that using AI tools often involves sharing data; review privacy policies to understand how your information is used and protected.

Next Steps

To solidify your understanding and gain practical experience, revisit the "Quick Win Exercise" in this chapter. Choose one of the suggested tools and spend a few minutes actively exploring its interface and capabilities. This hands-on interaction is the most effective way to build confidence and familiarity with AI. In the next chapter, we will begin to explore more specific ways you can use these tools to boost your productivity.

Chapter 3

AI Chatbots

Talking to Artificial Intelligence

Time to get practical. This chapter introduces AI chatbots - the tools that'll likely become part of your daily workflow. You've probably heard of ChatGPT. It's one of many chatbots available, including Claude (from Anthropic), Gemini (from Google), and Copilot (from Microsoft). Each has strengths we'll explore later. But first, let's understand what these tools actually do and how to use them effectively. Think of an AI chatbot as a text conversation with a knowledgeable assistant who never gets tired of your questions.

What is an AI Chatbot?

Imagine texting back and forth with a very smart friend who can answer your questions, help you write things, brainstorm ideas, and even tell you a joke. That's essentially what an AI chatbot is. It's designed to understand what you're saying and respond in a way that sounds like a real person.

You can:

- **Ask it questions:** "What's the capital of France?"
- **Give it instructions:** "Write a funny short story about a cat who travels the world."
- **Have a back-and-forth conversation with it:** "What

are some good restaurants in London?" then follow-up, e.g. "Are there any great vegetarian options near Heathrow Airport?"

Chatting is a simple but powerful way to interact with AI and get things done. The key is that it remembers the context of your conversation, so you can build on previous questions and answers.

How Chatbots Work: Language Models Made Simple

The core technology behind these chatbots is something called a "language model." This is a complex piece of technology, but we can explain it simply.

Think of a language model as a massive library inside the chatbot's brain. This library contains millions - or even billions - of books, articles, and websites. The chatbot has "read" everything in this library and, through this process, has learned how humans use language. It's like a super-smart friend who's absorbed a vast amount of knowledge about words, sentences, grammar, and context.

When you type something into a chatbot, it uses its language model to figure out what you mean. It then predicts the most likely and relevant words to form the best possible response. It's not "thinking" in the human sense, but rather calculating probabilities based on the patterns it has learned from all that data.

Your super-smart friend can instantly access all that information and give you the answer you're looking for, framed in a natural, conversational way.

Let's Get Practical: Using ChatGPT

Let's use ChatGPT as an example to see how AI chatbots work in practice. *If you haven't already created a free account on ChatGPT.com and downloaded the app, now is a good time to take a moment to do that.*

Here's a quick rundown of how to use ChatGPT:

Website:

1. Go to ChatGPT.com, sign up, and log in to your account.
2. You'll see a text box at the bottom of the screen. This is where you type in your "prompts" - your instructions or questions for the AI.
3. Once you've typed your prompt, click the arrow icon (or press Enter) to send it. ChatGPT will immediately start generating its response above the text box.

App:

1. Open the ChatGPT app on your phone or tablet.
2. You'll see a similar interface with a text box for your prompts.
3. The app has a handy microphone icon. You can tap this to use voice dictation instead of typing, which can be much faster and more natural, especially when you have a lot to say.
4. Many apps also offer a "voice mode" where you can have a spoken conversation with the AI, which feels very natural and can be great for brainstorming on the go.

Chatbot Capabilities: What They Can (and Can't) Do

AI chatbots can do some pretty amazing things. They're like multi-talented assistants who can help with various tasks:

- **Writing:** Need to draft an email, a letter, a report, an article, or even a poem? AI chatbots can help you generate creative text formats, tailor them to different writing styles, and even give you suggestions for improving your grammar and clarity. They can adapt to formal, informal, persuasive, or informative tones.
- **Brainstorming:** AI chatbots are excellent brainstorming partners. You can feed them a topic or a problem, and they can generate a wide range of ideas for projects, businesses, creative endeavours - pretty much anything you can imagine. They can help you explore different angles and perspectives.
- **Summarising:** Have a long document, article, or even a book chapter you need to understand quickly? AI chatbots can summarise the key points for you, extracting the most important information and presenting it concisely. This saves you valuable time and effort.
- **Answering Questions:** AI chatbots can answer your questions on a wide range of topics, providing information and explanations that are often surprisingly accurate and well-researched. They can act as a quick reference tool for facts, concepts, or definitions.
- **Translating:** Need to translate text from one

language to another? Many AI chatbots can handle this quickly and accurately, making global communication easier.

- **Coding Assistance:** While this book isn't about coding, it's worth noting that AI chatbots can also help with basic coding tasks, debugging, or explaining programming concepts.

Example: Let's say you need to write a quick email to a client. You could ask ChatGPT: "Write a professional email to [Client Name] thanking them for their recent order and confirming the delivery date."

Example: If you're brainstorming ideas for a new business, you could ask ChatGPT: "Give me 10 creative business ideas for a service that helps people with [specific problem]?"

Example: You're reading a lengthy research article about the benefits of plant-based diets. You could ask ChatGPT: "Summarise the main arguments in this research article about the benefits of plant-based diets."

Example: If you're handling a sensitive situation with a client, such as when their project has been delayed due to a bereavement, you could ask ChatGPT: "How do I respond to the client's interest in moving forward while being respectful and sensitive to their recent loss?" The AI can help you craft empathetic and professional language.

What Can't AI Chatbots Do (Yet!)?

AI chatbots are amazing, but they're not perfect. While they're getting better all the time, they still have some limitations. It's important to understand these so you can use them effectively and avoid frustration.

Here are a few things AI chatbots might struggle with:

- **Common Sense:** AI chatbots lack the common sense that we humans take for granted. They operate based on patterns in data, not real-world understanding. This means they can misinterpret your requests if you aren't clear and specific. They won't "read between the lines" in the same way a human would.

- **Emotions and Empathy:** They can't genuinely understand or express emotions. Don't expect them to offer a shoulder to cry on or truly empathise with your feelings (although they might try to offer words of comfort based on patterns of empathetic language they've learned).

- **Complex Reasoning:** While some AI chatbots are getting very good at complex reasoning and problem-solving, this is still an area where AI is rapidly evolving. They might struggle with nuanced ethical dilemmas, philosophical questions, or tasks requiring deep, original critical thinking that goes beyond pattern recognition. It's important to remember that even the most advanced AI systems aren't perfect thinkers yet.

- **Real-time, Up-to-date Information (sometimes):** Many AI models have a "knowledge cut-off" date. This means they only know about information up to a certain point in time, just like a book or a newspaper that was printed last year. Always verify critical or time-sensitive information with a reliable, current source.

- **Originality and Creativity (to a degree):** While AI can generate creative text, it does so by remixing and combining existing patterns. True human originality, intuition, and groundbreaking innovation are still beyond its current capabilities. It can be a great assistant for creativity, but it's not a replacement for it.

- **Personal Experience:** AI has no personal experiences, beliefs, or consciousness. Its responses are based purely on the data it was trained on. It can't offer genuine personal anecdotes or truly understand subjective human experiences.

Example: You ask ChatGPT, "How can I make a million pounds?" The chatbot might give you a list of business ideas or financial strategies, but it won't understand the complexities of achieving financial success, which requires much more than just a good idea - it involves market conditions, personal drive, networking, and often a bit of luck. It can't give you a guaranteed path to wealth because it doesn't understand the real-world variables.

The Art of Prompting: Giving Instructions to AI

To use AI effectively, we need to know how to talk to it. This is where "prompting" comes in. A prompt is simply the instruction or question you give to the AI. It's how you tell it what you want it to do.

The better your prompts, the better the results you'll get. If you don't provide specific, well-crafted instructions, you might end up with a jumbled mess of words instead of a helpful response. It's like trying to ask for directions without really knowing where you want to go - you'll end up lost, or at least not where you intended!

How to Approach Prompting

There are three main ways to think about crafting prompts, and you'll likely use a mix of them:

1. **Simple Prompting:** Start simple! For everyday tasks, just tell the AI what you need in a straightforward way. You don't always need to craft a super-detailed prompt. For example, "Write a short email to my team about the holiday party."

2. **Conversational Prompting:** This is how I do it most of the time. I use voice dictation to give long, detailed instructions to the AI, just as if I'm talking to a colleague. This allows me to provide a lot of context naturally and adjust the prompt as I go, building on previous responses. It feels very natural and efficient.

3. **Structured Prompting:** We'll cover this in more depth in the next chapter, but essentially it involves using a framework to create consistent and precise prompts. This is particularly useful for complex or repetitive tasks where you need very specific outputs.

Tips for Better Prompting

Crafting effective prompts is a skill that significantly improves your AI interactions. For now, the most important thing to remember is to be clear and specific when you tell the AI what you want it to do. Generally, the more relevant context you provide, the better the outcome will be.

We dedicate the entire next chapter, 'The Art of Prompting,' to this vital skill. There, we'll explore frameworks like the GOAL method and many more specific techniques to help you get precisely what you need from the AI. So, for now, experiment with giving clear instructions, and get ready to level up your prompting game very soon!

Your Quick Win: Try One Task with Three Different Prompts

Choose a task you want to do with AI, like writing a social media post or generating ideas for a blog post. Write three different prompts for that task, experimenting with different levels of detail and see how the AI's responses change based on your instructions.

1. **Prompt 1 (Simple):** "Write a social media post about [your topic]."

2. **Prompt 2 (More Detail):** "Write a social media post for [platform, e.g., LinkedIn] about [your topic]. Make it [tone, e.g., encouraging] and include [specific call to action]."

3. **Prompt 3 (Structured/Role-based):** "Act as a [role, e.g., small business marketing consultant]. Write a social media post for [platform] about [your topic]. The post should be [length/format, e.g., 100 words, 3 bullet points]. Focus on [key benefit] and include a call to action to [specific action]."

Compare the outputs. Notice how adding more detail and structure guides the AI to produce more relevant and useful results.

By mastering these prompting techniques, you'll be well on your way to becoming an AI power user, unlocking the potential of these tools to enhance your work and personal life.

Key Takeaways

- AI chatbots are conversational programs that mimic human interaction.
- They use "language models" to understand and generate responses based on vast data.
- Popular chatbots include ChatGPT, Claude, Gemini, and Copilot.
- Chatbots can help with writing, brainstorming, summarising, and answering questions.
- Limitations include lack of common sense, emotions, and sometimes real-time information.
- "Prompting" - giving clear instructions - is key to getting good results.
- Experiment with simple, conversational, and structured prompting.

Next Steps

Before moving on, spend some time experimenting with the prompts you created in the exercise. Try refining them further. What happens if you ask the AI to be more concise? Or more creative? The more you play, the more you'll learn about how to get the AI to work for you.

Chapter 4

The Art of Prompting

Giving Clear Instructions to AI

Getting useful results from AI comes down to an important skill: writing clear instructions.

In the last chapter, you learned to chat with AI. Now we'll make those chats productive. I'll introduce the GOAL framework - a simple method for crafting prompts that get you exactly what you need.

Vague instructions waste time and don't get you the results you need. Specific instructions work far better, saving you time and getting you better results. The difference between "write a blog post to market my business" and a well-crafted prompt is the difference between generic fluff and content you can actually use.

If you don't provide specific, well-crafted instructions, you might get an unhelpful mess of words instead of a useful response. It's not that the AI is "bad"; it's just doing its best with the information you've given it.

What is a Prompt?

A prompt is simply a question, statement, or set of instructions that you give to an AI chatbot. It's the starting point of your conversation.

The clearer and more specific your prompt, the better the AI can understand your needs and give you a useful response.

Let's look at some examples to see how prompts can be improved:

Example:

- **Vague Prompt:** "Write about dogs."
    - *Why it's vague:* This gives the AI very little to go on. It could write about anything related to dogs - their history, different breeds, how to care for them, or even a fictional story. The output will likely be generic and not what you need.
- **More Specific Prompt:** "Write a list of the 10 most popular dog breeds in the UK."
    - *Why it's better:* This prompt specifies the topic (dog breeds), the quantity (10), the format (a list), and the region (UK). This will give you a much more focused and useful response.
- **Even Better Prompt:** "I'm writing a blog post for new dog owners about the best dog breeds for families with young children. Create a table listing the top 5 dog breeds for families, including information about their temperament, size, and exercise needs. Also, suggest a few reputable sources where I can find more information about these breeds, such as kennel club websites or well-known animal welfare organisations."
    - *Why it's excellent:* This prompt provides a clear goal (blog post for new dog owners), defines the audience (families with young children), specifies the output format (table), details the required information for each entry (temperament, size, exercise needs), and even asks for additional resources with specific criteria. This leaves

very little room for misinterpretation and will generate a highly relevant and actionable response.

Notice how the prompts become increasingly detailed and specific. This helps the AI understand exactly what you're looking for and generate a more relevant and valuable response.

It's about guiding the AI, not just asking it a question.

The GOAL Framework: Your Guide to Effective Instructions

Here's a simple framework - the GOAL framework - to help you craft better instructions for AI. Using this framework will help you think through all the necessary components of a good prompt.

- **G - Goal:** Clearly define what you want to achieve. What's the end goal of this interaction? What specific information or output are you hoping to get? Be precise about your objective.
    - *Example:* "I need to draft a persuasive email to a potential client."
- **O - Output:** Tell the AI what format you want the response in. Do you need a list, a table, a paragraph, a poem, a piece of code, a summary, or something else? Specifying the format helps the AI structure its response correctly.
    - *Example:* "The email should be concise, no more than 150 words, and include a clear call to action."
- **A - Additional Context:** Think about any background information that would help the AI

understand your request better. What's the purpose of the task? Who is your target audience? What specific details are essential for the AI to know? The more context, the better.

  - *Example:* "The client is [Client Name], a small business owner in the [industry] sector. We're offering [your service/product] which helps them [solve specific problem]. I want to highlight [key benefit 1] and [key benefit 2]."

- **L - Look at the Output:** Always review the AI's response critically. Does it meet your expectations? Is the information accurate and relevant? Does it answer all parts of your question? Is the tone right? If not, don't hesitate to rephrase your prompt, add more context, or ask follow-up questions to refine the output. This iterative process is crucial for getting the best results.

  - *Example:* After getting the email draft, you might notice it's too formal. Your "Look" step would involve asking: "Can you rewrite that email in a slightly more friendly and conversational tone?"

Let's apply the GOAL framework to a common scenario: You're planning a trip to Paris and need help creating an itinerary.

Prompt using GOAL:

- **Goal:** "I want to create a 3-day itinerary for a trip to Paris."

- **Output:** "I need a list of activities and attractions for each day, formatted as a daily schedule, including estimated times, transportation details (e.g., walking, Metro lines), and approximate costs for entry fees."

- **Additional Context:** "I'm traveling with my partner. We're interested in history, art, food, and exploring local neighbourhoods. We have a moderate budget and enjoy walking. We prefer to avoid overly touristy traps where possible and find some local gems. We'll be staying near the Latin Quarter."
- **Look:** Check the output. See if the attractions are actually open at the suggested times, and double-check other details like whether booking is required, current prices, and if the transportation suggestions are practical. You might also ask for restaurant recommendations in the areas suggested.

Tips for Better Instructions

Here are a few more tips that can help you get better results from AI:

- **Start with a simple instruction and add detail as needed:** Don't feel you have to get it perfect on the first try. You can always refine your instruction based on the initial response. It's a conversation, not a one-off command.
- **Don't be afraid to use voice dictation:** Especially on mobile devices, speaking your prompts can be much quicker and more natural than typing, allowing you to provide more detailed context without effort.
- **Create templates for tasks you do frequently:** If you often write similar types of emails, social media posts, or reports, create a basic prompt template you can reuse. Just fill in the specifics each time. This

saves time and makes your outputs more consistent.

- **If you're working with a team, share your best instructions:** When you discover a prompt that works really well for a specific task, share it with your colleagues. This can help everyone get better results from AI and ensure consistency across your business or projects.

- **Be Explicit About Tone and Style:** If you want the AI to write in a specific tone (e.g., friendly, formal, humorous, authoritative) or style (e.g., journalistic, academic, conversational), tell it. "Write this in a friendly, encouraging tone."

- **Provide Examples (Few-Shot Learning):** If you have a specific style or format in mind, provide one or two examples of what you're looking for. This is incredibly powerful. For instance, "Here are two examples of social media posts I like. Write a new one in a similar style."

- **Iterate and Refine:** Don't settle for the first answer. If the AI's response isn't quite right, tell it what you want to change. "Make it shorter," "Expand on point number three," or "Can you rephrase that to be more direct?"

- **Break Down Complex Tasks:** For very large or complex tasks, break them down into smaller, manageable steps. Guide the AI through each step rather than asking it to do everything at once. For example, first ask for an outline, then ask it to write each section based on that outline.

Exercise

Let's put these prompting skills into practice. Choose a task relevant to your work or personal life that you think AI could help with. For example, drafting a client email, creating a social media post, or summarising a long article.

Now, using the GOAL framework, craft a detailed prompt for that task.

- **G - Goal:** What exactly do you want to achieve?
- **O - Output:** What format should the AI's response take?
- **A - Additional Context:** What background information or specific details does the AI need to know?
- **L - Look at the Output:** (This is your mental step after the AI responds).

Once you've crafted your prompt, try it out in ChatGPT (or your preferred chatbot). Then, critically review the output. What worked well? What could be improved? Try refining your prompt based on your observations.

By mastering these prompting techniques, you'll be well on your way to becoming an AI power user, unlocking the potential of these tools to enhance your work and personal life.

This skill of prompting is arguably the most important one you'll develop in your AI journey.

Key Takeaways:

- Clear, specific prompts are essential for getting useful AI responses.

- The GOAL framework (Goal, Output, Additional Context, Look at the Output) helps structure effective prompts.
- Provide as much relevant detail and context as possible.
- Specify the desired format, tone, and style.
- Iterate and refine your prompts based on the AI's responses.
- Breaking down complex tasks into smaller steps can improve results.

Next Steps

Continue experimenting with the GOAL framework. Pick another task from your daily routine and try to apply the framework to create a prompt. The more you practice, the more intuitive it will become. Pay attention to how small changes in your prompt can lead to big differences in the AI's output.

Chapter 5

More Advanced AI Techniques

You've got the basics down. You know how to chat with AI and write effective prompts. What's next?

This chapter explores three advanced techniques: fine-tuning AI for your specific needs, building Custom GPTs for repeated tasks, and combining tools into automated workflows.

These might sound complex, but they're becoming more accessible every month. I'll show you exactly when each technique makes sense for your business.

Fine-Tuning: Training AI Your Way

Imagine having an AI that's been specially trained to understand your business, your unique writing style, your specific industry jargon, or even your favourite recipes. That's the power of "fine-tuning."

Think of it like this: you buy a brand new phone, but it does not have any of your contacts, photos, or apps on it. It is pretty useless until you personalise it, right? You add your data, set your preferences, and make it truly *yours*.

Fine-tuning is similar. We take a pre-trained AI model, such as the powerful language models that run ChatGPT, and train it further on your own specific data. This could be anything from your company's internal documents, your past client communications, your personal writing samples, a collection of industry reports, or even your family recipes. By feeding the AI your unique information, you are teaching it to think and respond in a way that is tailored precisely to your specific needs and context.

Why is this so valuable for independent professionals?

- **Increased Accuracy and Relevance:** By learning from your data, the AI becomes much more accurate and relevant to your specific tasks. It is less likely to make mistakes or give you generic, useless answers because it understands *your* world.

- **Customised Solutions:** You can create AI tools that are specifically designed for your niche industry, your unique business processes, or even your personal hobbies. This means the AI can speak your language and understand your specific challenges.

- **Competitive Edge:** Fine-tuned AI can give you a significant advantage in your work or business. It allows you to automate tasks, generate content, or analyse information in ways that others cannot do as easily or as effectively with generic AI tools. It is like having a highly specialised assistant who only works for you.

- **Consistency:** If you need AI to produce content or responses that consistently match your brand voice or specific terminology, fine-tuning can ensure that consistency across all outputs.

While true "fine-tuning" often requires some technical know-how, the good news is that many AI platforms are making it easier to achieve similar results through user-friendly interfaces, often referred to as "Custom GPTs" or similar features.

Custom GPTs: Building Your Own AI Tools

Those "language models" we talked about - the ones that power chatbots such as ChatGPT - many platforms now allow you to build your own AI tools, often called "Custom GPTs" (a feature available within ChatGPT Plus) or similar custom AI assistants. These are essentially mini versions of a powerful AI chatbot that are "fine-tuned" or configured to be experts in a specific area, using your instructions and data.

Imagine being able to create:

- **A Custom GPT for summarising legal documents:** You could train it on thousands of contracts and legal texts, teaching it to extract key clauses, identify risks, or summarise case precedents quickly and accurately. This would be invaluable for a legal consultant.

- **A Custom GPT for writing marketing copy:** This AI could be trained on your successful past campaigns, your company's brand guidelines, and your target audience's preferences. It would then generate marketing copy that perfectly matches your voice and objectives.

- **A Custom GPT for generating meal plans:** You could feed it your dietary preferences, allergies, and the ingredients you have on hand, and it would create personalised meal plans and shopping lists.

- **A Custom GPT for client onboarding:** This AI could be loaded with all your onboarding documents, FAQs, and processes, allowing it to answer new client questions consistently and efficiently, freeing up your time.

- **A Custom GPT for niche research:** If you specialise in a very specific industry, you could train an AI on all the relevant reports, articles, and data in that field, making it an unparalleled research assistant for your niche.

The possibilities are vast! You can create a Custom GPT for almost any task where you need a highly specialised AI assistant. These tools are becoming increasingly user-friendly, often requiring no coding, just clear instructions and relevant data.

Combining AI Tools: The Power of Integration

AI tools can be even more powerful when they work together. Think of it like assembling a team of specialists, each with their own unique skills. By connecting different AI tools, you can create seamless workflows that automate complex tasks and save you a significant amount of time and effort. This is often referred to as "AI integration" or "workflow automation."

Here is a practical example of how you might combine AI tools:

1. **You use the Otter.ai app (or a similar transcription service) to record a client meeting or a brainstorming session.** Otter.ai automatically generates a highly accurate transcript of the conversation in real-time.

2. **You copy and paste that transcript into ChatGPT (or another AI chatbot).**

3. **You then ask ChatGPT to perform several tasks based on the transcript:**

    - "Summarise the key discussion points from this

meeting."

- "Create a list of action items, assigning them to specific people mentioned in the transcript."
- "Draft a follow-up email to everyone who attended the meeting, including the summary and action items."
- "Identify any potential client objections or concerns raised during the discussion."

By integrating these two AI tools - a transcription service and a powerful chatbot - you have automated a process that could have taken you hours to do manually. You have gone from a raw audio recording to a summarised meeting, action items, and a draft email, all in a matter of minutes.

Other examples of integration include:

- **AI for Content Repurposing:** Use an AI writing tool to generate a long-form article, then feed it into another AI tool (or the same one with a new prompt) to create social media posts, email snippets, and video scripts from that single article.
- **AI for Data Analysis and Reporting:** Use an AI tool to extract key data points from a spreadsheet, then use another AI to generate a concise report or presentation summary based on that data.
- **AI for Customer Support:** Combine an AI chatbot with your customer relationship management (CRM) system to automatically answer common customer questions, freeing up your time for more complex inquiries.

The key is to identify repetitive tasks in your workflow and see if there are multiple AI tools that, when chained together, can automate the entire process. This is where the real productivity gains happen.

Exercise

Think about a task you do regularly in your work or personal life. This could be something at work, a personal project, or even just a hobby. Now consider how you could use the advanced AI techniques discussed in this chapter to make that task easier, faster, or more creative:

- Could you create a Custom GPT specifically for that task? What kind of data would it need to be "trained" on (or configured with)?
- Could you combine different AI tools to automate parts of the process? What tools would you use, and in what order?

Write down your ideas. The goal is to start thinking creatively about how advanced AI techniques can be applied to real-world problems and how they can give you a significant advantage. Even if you do not implement these ideas right away, the act of thinking through them will deepen your understanding of AI's potential.

Key Takeaways:

- **Fine-tuning** allows you to train AI models on your specific data for increased accuracy and customisation.
- **Custom GPTs** are tailored AI assistants built for specific tasks, often without coding.

- **Combining AI tools** through integration creates powerful, automated workflows.
- Look for opportunities to automate multi-step tasks by chaining different AI capabilities.
- These advanced techniques offer a significant competitive edge and productivity boost.

Next Steps

Take one of the ideas you brainstormed in the exercise and research if there is an existing AI tool or platform that offers "Custom GPT" or similar customisation features. Explore how you might start building your own specialised AI assistant for that task. Even if it is just a basic setup, the hands-on experience will be invaluable.

Chapter 6

Setting Up Your AI Workspace

When you're starting out, trying too many AI tools can be overwhelming, and create chaos instead of clarity. This chapter helps you build a workspace that actually works for you.

You'll learn which accounts to create first, how to organise your tools, and ways to integrate AI into your existing systems. By the end, you'll have a system that makes AI a natural part of your daily routine, not an added burden.

Your Quick Win: Create Your Dedicated AI Workspace Folder

Before we dive into tools, let's get a quick win. This simple action takes less than a minute and immediately starts bringing order to your AI efforts.

1. **On your computer, create a new main folder.** Name it something clear, like AI_Workspace.
2. **Inside AI_Workspace, create three sub-folders:**
    - Prompts (for prompts that generate great results)
    - Outputs (for all the content AI creates for you)
    - Templates (for any reusable structures or guidelines you develop)

That's it. You now have a central hub for all your AI-related files. This small step prevents future clutter and sets the stage for a highly organised workflow.

Creating Your Core AI Accounts (The Foundation)

Setting up AI tools does not require technical expertise - it requires a systematic approach. Most professionals I work with get overwhelmed because they try to set up everything at once. Instead, start with three core platforms that handle 80% of your AI needs.

The Problem: Drafting emails, reports, and social media posts takes too long.

The Solution: Use a powerful text-based AI. For most of us, written communication consumes a large part of the day. Drafting emails, proposals, marketing copy, or even internal reports can be a significant time sink. This is where a text-based AI assistant becomes your primary tool.

Start with ChatGPT Plus or Claude Pro. These are your primary text-based AI assistants. Choose one - do not try to use both initially. I recommend ChatGPT Plus for most professionals because it integrates with more tools and has broader capability. The monthly cost of around $/£/€20 should pay for itself within days or even hours when you factor in time savings – and become more proficient with the tools.

- **Case Study: Alex, a freelance marketing consultant.** Alex used to spend hours brainstorming blog post ideas and writing initial drafts. After subscribing to ChatGPT Plus, she found she could generate a detailed outline in 10 minutes and a complete first draft in 30, cutting her content creation time by more than half.

Create your account using your business email address, not a personal one. The key benefit is that you will separate your professional AI usage from personal usage. Use a strong, unique password, and enable two-factor authentication for more security.

The Problem: Creating engaging visuals for marketing and presentations is time-consuming and expensive.

The Solution: Add a visual AI tool. In today's digital world, compelling visuals are no longer optional. Whether it's for social media, presentations, or website content, generating high-quality images can be a bottleneck for independent professionals without a dedicated design team.

Add a visual AI tool next. For most business applications, this means either Midjourney or DALL-E (which comes with ChatGPT Plus). If you are creating marketing materials, presentations, or social media content, visual AI will become essential to your workflow.

- **Case Study: Ben, a small business owner.** Ben struggled to create unique images for his online course materials. He started using Midjourney and now generates custom graphics in minutes, saving him hundreds in stock photo subscriptions and design fees.

The Problem: You spend too much time transcribing meetings or voice notes.

The Solution: Set up a voice AI tool. For consultants, coaches, and anyone who conducts frequent calls or brainstorms ideas aloud, the manual transcription of audio can be a huge drain on time. Converting spoken words into actionable text is a key pain point.

Set up a voice AI tool. Tools such as Otter.ai or Whisper (also from OpenAI) can transcribe meetings, phone calls, and voice memos. This is particularly valuable for consultants and coaches who conduct client calls regularly.

Case Study: Anya, a leadership coach. *Anya used to hand-write notes during client sessions, often missing key details. With Otter.ai, she can record calls - with client permission – get a full transcription, and easily pull out action items and insights for her follow-up reports. This has significantly improved her client service and reduced post-session workload.*

The key principle here is progressive setup. Master one tool before adding the next. Each tool should solve a specific problem in your current workflow.

Guiding Questions:

- Identify three specific tasks in your current workflow that consume significant time and could potentially benefit from AI.
- List your daily activities that primarily involve writing, visual creation, or voice processing.
- Pinpoint repetitive tasks you perform regularly that could be automated with AI.
- What is your current budget for professional tools, and how does this compare to the potential time savings from AI?

- Do you prefer to master one tool deeply before moving to the next, or do you find value in experimenting with multiple options simultaneously?

Organising Your AI Workflow (The System)

Once you have your core accounts, the next challenge is organisation. Without a system, you will waste time switching between tools, forgetting passwords, and losing track of your AI conversations and outputs. This is a common hurdle: studies show that up to 30% of professionals report losing significant time each week due to disorganised digital files.

Create a dedicated AI workspace on your computer. This means a specific folder structure where you save AI outputs, prompts that work well, and templates you develop. I use a simple structure: AI_Workspace > Prompts > Outputs > Templates. This takes five minutes to set up but saves hours later.

- **Case Study: Mark, a financial advisor.** Mark initially saved AI-generated content haphazardly. He spent valuable time searching for past reports or useful prompt responses. After setting up his AI_Workspace folder structure, he could instantly locate client summaries and market analyses, saving him an average of 30 minutes per day.

Use a password manager if you do not already. Tools such as 1Password or Bitwarden become essential when you are managing multiple AI accounts. You will also want to store API keys securely if you start using more advanced integrations.

Set up browser bookmarks or shortcuts. Create a bookmark folder called "AI Tools" and organise your most-used platforms there. This eliminates the friction of remembering URLs or searching for login pages.

Establish a naming convention for your AI projects. Whether you are generating marketing copy, analysing data, or creating presentations, consistent naming helps you find previous work quickly. Use whatever format you want, but keep it consistent.

The goal is to make AI tools feel like natural extensions of your existing workflow, not additional complexity. The easier it is to access and use these tools, the more likely you are to actually use them consistently.

Guiding Questions:

- Describe your current system for organising digital files and projects. Where are the pain points?
- How do you currently manage passwords and accounts for your professional tools? Are there any security gaps?
- Reflect on the last month: how often did you struggle to find a previous project or an important digital asset?
- When are you most productive? How can your AI workspace support your focus during these times?
- How do you prefer to access frequently-used tools - through browser bookmarks, desktop shortcuts, or mobile apps?

Testing and Optimising Your Setup (The Validation)

The difference between a functional AI workspace and an optimised one lies in testing and refinement. Most people set up their tools and never revisit the configuration. This is a missed opportunity for significant productivity gains.

Run a week-long test of your core workflow. Choose three typical tasks from your regular work and complete them using your new AI setup. Track the time taken and note any friction points. This baseline measurement becomes crucial for optimising your approach.

Document what works and what does not. Keep a simple log of successful prompts, useful outputs, and frustrating experiences. After a week, you will see patterns that inform how to adjust your setup.

Adjust your tool selection based on actual usage. You might discover that you rarely use the visual AI tool but constantly need better writing assistance. Or you might find that voice transcription saves you more time than expected. Let real usage data guide your tool choices, not marketing promises.

Create your first set of templates and shortcuts. Based on your testing week, develop 3-5 prompt templates for your most common tasks. These become the foundation of your AI productivity system.

This testing phase is where many professionals either become AI power users or abandon the tools entirely. The key is honest evaluation - if a tool does not save you time or improve your output quality within two weeks, either adjust how you are using it or replace it with something else.

Guiding Questions:

- Pinpoint the three most time-consuming tasks in your typical work week. These are your prime candidates for AI.
- What specific metrics will you use to measure if AI tools are genuinely saving you time or improving your output quality?
- Envision success: what would AI integration look like in your specific role or business within the next three months?
- How willing are you to experiment with and adjust digital tools based on real-world experience?
- What is your backup plan if the initial AI setup doesn't immediately deliver the expected results?

Key Takeaways

1. **Start with three core tools** - Address common pain points by choosing ChatGPT Plus (or Claude Pro) for text, a visual AI platform for graphics, and a voice AI tool for transcription. Master one before adding others.
2. **Create a systematic workspace** - Implement dedicated folders, consistent naming conventions, and organised bookmarks to prevent AI tools from adding chaos to your workflow. An organised workspace is critical for long-term productivity.
3. **Test and refine based on real usage** - Run a week-long test of your core workflow with AI. This practical evaluation reveals more about tool

effectiveness than months of theoretical planning, guiding your adjustments.

Your Next Action

Choose your first AI tool and create the account today. Set up your basic folder structure (AI_Workspace > Prompts > Outputs > Templates) and bookmark the platform. Tomorrow, identify one specific task from your regular workflow and complete it using AI assistance. Track the time and quality compared to your usual approach.

The biggest barrier to AI adoption is not learning the tools - it is overcoming the initial setup friction. Once your workspace is configured and tested, AI becomes a natural part of how you work rather than an additional burden.

Chapter 7

AI Troubleshooting

Dealing with Errors

AI makes mistakes. Sometimes it misunderstands. Sometimes it invents facts. This is normal.

This chapter teaches you to spot errors, verify information, and fix common problems. You'll learn why AI gets things wrong and how to get better results when it does.

Understanding these limitations makes you a more effective AI user. This chapter is all about dealing with those moments when AI goes a bit off-track and how to become a more confident, effective AI user by knowing how to fix things.

AI Errors: Don't Panic!

If you're getting strange, incorrect, or just plain weird responses from your AI, don't worry! It happens to all of us, even experienced AI users. It doesn't mean you're doing something wrong, and it certainly doesn't mean AI is useless. It simply means we need to understand *why* AI makes these mistakes and, more importantly, *how to fix them*. Think of it as a learning curve - for both you and the AI.

Why AI Gets Things Wrong

Remember how we talked about language models earlier? AI chatbots use these models to understand your prompts and generate responses. These models are trained on vast amounts of data from the internet, books, articles, and other sources. While this data is immense, it isn't always perfect, unbiased, or completely up-to-date.

Here are a few common reasons why AI might get things wrong:

- **Reasoning Limitations (Hallucinations):** AI is excellent at finding patterns and generating text that *sounds* plausible, but it can struggle with complex reasoning, logic problems, or tasks that require genuine understanding of the real world. Sometimes, AI will confidently make up facts or provide incorrect information - this is often called "hallucinating." It might make a mistake if your request involves multiple steps, requires abstract concepts, or demands a deep, nuanced understanding that goes beyond pattern matching.

- **Limited Context Window:** AI chatbots have a limited "memory." They can only "remember" a certain number of previous messages in a conversation. This is called the "context window." If the conversation gets too long, the AI might "forget" what you were talking about earlier and start giving irrelevant or repetitive answers. It's like trying to have a long conversation with someone who has a very short-term memory.

- **Bias in Training Data:** AI models can reflect biases present in their training data. For example, if an AI has been trained mostly on text written by a particular demographic or from a specific cultural perspective, it might have trouble understanding or responding appropriately to prompts related to other experiences. This can lead to unfair, inaccurate, or even offensive outputs.

- **Ambiguous Prompts:** As we discussed in the previous chapter, if your prompt is vague, unclear, or contains conflicting instructions, the AI will struggle to give you a good answer. It can't read your mind, so it will try its best to interpret what you mean, which often leads to less-than-ideal results.
- **Lack of Real-time Information:** Many AI models have a "knowledge cut-off" date. This means they might not have information about very recent events, new research, or the latest trends. If you ask about something that happened last week, the AI might not know about it and could provide outdated information or even make something up.

Fact-Checking: The Essential AI Skill

AI can be a great source of information, a powerful research assistant, and a fantastic content generator. However, you should never blindly trust everything it tells you. **Always double-check any facts or claims, especially if they're important for your work, business decisions, or anything that requires accuracy.** This is perhaps the most essential skill you'll develop as an AI user.

Here are a few ways to fact-check AI-generated information:

- **Compare with Other Sources:** Look for the same information on trusted websites, in reputable books, academic journals, or from well-known experts in the field. Cross-referencing is your best friend.
- **Examine Citations (if provided):** Some AI tools or plugins can provide links to their sources. If so,

make sure those sources are credible and directly support the AI's claims. Don't just assume a link means the information is correct - click through and verify.

- **Use Your Common Sense and Expertise:** Does the information sound too good to be true? Does it contradict something you already know to be accurate based on your experience? If so, be sceptical and investigate further. Your own knowledge is a powerful filter.

- **Perform Targeted Web Searches:** If the AI gives you a specific statistic or claim, copy and paste it into a search engine to see if you can find independent verification.

Troubleshooting Tips: Your AI Repair Toolkit

Here's a toolkit to help you fix those AI errors and get the responses you need:

- **Rephrase Your Prompts:** This is often the simplest and most effective solution. If the AI isn't giving you what you want, try rephrasing your prompt. Experiment with different ways of asking the same question, using different keywords or sentence structures. Sometimes, a slight change in wording can make all the difference.

- **Break Down Complex Tasks:** If your prompt is too complicated or asks the AI to do too many things at once, break it into smaller, more manageable steps. Give the AI one instruction at a time, and build upon its responses. For example, instead of "Write a full marketing plan for my new business," try "First, give me an outline for a marketing plan," then "Now, write the section on target audience," and so on.

- **Provide More Context:** The more information you give the AI, the better it can understand your request and give you a relevant answer. Think about the "Additional Context" part of the GOAL framework. What background information, constraints, or examples can you provide to guide the AI?

- **Specify the Output Format:** If you want a list, ask for a list. If you want a table, ask for a table. Being explicit about the desired format can prevent the AI from giving you a long paragraph when you needed bullet points.

- **Define the AI's Role:** Tell the AI what persona it should adopt. "Act as a seasoned business consultant," or "You are a creative writer." This helps the AI tailor its tone, style, and knowledge base.

- **Start a New Chat:** Sometimes, the best solution is to start fresh. If the AI seems confused, keeps giving you irrelevant responses, or has "forgotten" earlier parts of a long conversation, simply open a new chat window and rephrase your request from scratch. This clears its "memory" and gives it a clean slate.

- **Experiment with Different AI Models:** If one AI chatbot isn't performing well for a specific task, try another. ChatGPT, Claude, and Gemini each have their strengths and weaknesses. What works well in one might not work as well in another.

- **Give Examples (Few-Shot Prompting):** If you have a very specific style or type of output you're looking for, provide one or two examples within your prompt. This is a powerful way to guide the AI. For instance, "Here are two examples of how I write client emails. Please draft a new email in a similar style."

Exercise

Let's put your troubleshooting skills to the test. Try the "Sally" problem (or a similar logic puzzle if you prefer). Type this into the AI:

"Sally has three brothers. Each brother has two sisters. How many sisters does Sally have?"

1. **Try solving this logic puzzle with ChatGPT or Claude.** See if you can guide the AI to the correct answer by providing clear, step-by-step instructions. You might need to break down the problem, ask clarifying questions, or even correct the AI if it makes a mistake.

2. **Now, try a similar logic puzzle with a different AI tool.** Do you get the same result? Does one AI handle logic better than another?

This exercise will help you understand how different AIs approach reasoning and why it's always important to verify their outputs, especially for tasks requiring precise logic or factual accuracy. It also reinforces the idea that you are the guide, and the AI is your tool.

Key Takeaways:

- AI errors are common and usually stem from reasoning limitations, limited context, or biased training data.

- **Fact-checking** AI-generated information is crucial - always verify critical details.
- Troubleshooting involves **rephrasing prompts, breaking down tasks, providing more context, specifying output, defining roles, and starting new chats.**
- Experimenting with different AI models can yield better results for specific tasks.
- Your role is to guide and verify the AI's output, not just accept it.

Next Steps

Next time you use an AI tool and don't get the result you expect, don't give up! Instead, apply one or two of the troubleshooting tips from this chapter. Try rephrasing your prompt, adding more context, or breaking the task into smaller steps. Notice how these adjustments change the AI's response and help you get closer to your desired outcome.

Chapter 8

Smart and Simple AI Privacy

Your data matters. When you use AI tools, you're sharing information - sometimes sensitive information.

This chapter introduces the AI-Powered Data Privacy Matrix™, a simple framework I developed to help AI users decide what's safe to share and what isn't. You'll learn to categorise both AI systems and data types, making privacy decisions clearer.

Protecting your information is a key part of using AI tools responsibly. While the idea of data privacy might sound technical or overwhelming at first, it doesn't have to be. In fact, with just a few clear guidelines, you can avoid most of the common pitfalls. This chapter will show you how to make smart, confident choices about your data – without needing a legal or technical background.

Why Data Privacy Matters

When you're interacting with AI systems you're providing data, either directly through your prompts or indirectly through your usage patterns. Some of this data may include personal details, sensitive business information, or legally protected data like health records or client financial details. The risks of mishandling this data can range from data breaches where your information is exposed to legal liabilities under laws like the GDPR (General Data Protection Regulation in Europe) or HIPAA (Health

Insurance Portability and Accountability Act in the US), depending on where you're operating and the nature of the data.

Beyond legal compliance, data privacy also impacts trust. Your clients, customers, or colleagues need to know that their information is safe when you use AI tools. If they feel their data is at risk, you could lose credibility, and it's incredibly difficult to regain trust once it's lost. Protecting data isn't just about rules; it's about maintaining your professional reputation and client relationships.

The AI-Powered Data Privacy Matrix™

To help you manage this complex area, I've created a simple framework called the AI-Powered Data Privacy Matrix™. This tool categorises AI systems based on their privacy features and sorts data types by sensitivity. It gives you a straightforward way to determine what kind of data is safe to input into different AI tools, helping you make informed decisions quickly.

Let's break down the core elements of the matrix and how you can use it.

Understanding AI Systems and Privacy

There are two major types of AI systems when it comes to privacy: **Private AI** and **Non-Private AI**.

- **Private AI**: These systems are designed *not* to use your input data for training their underlying models. This means that whatever you input stays within your session or your private instance of the system and isn't stored or shared for future use by the AI provider to improve their general models.

- **Examples:**
  - **Self-hosted AI:** This runs on your own hardware or private cloud infrastructure. You have maximum control because the data never leaves your system.
  - **Paid AI services with strong, transparent data handling policies:** Many enterprise-level AI services or paid tiers of popular tools offer "opt-out" options for data training or guarantee that your data won't be used for training. They often have clear privacy policies that explicitly state this.
  - **Local AI models:** Some AI models can run entirely on your device (e.g., on your computer or phone) without sending any data to the cloud.

- **Non-Private AI:** On the other hand, these systems *may* use your data for further training or store it for other purposes. These systems are usually free or have unclear data usage policies. Most free online AI tools, especially public chatbots, fall into this category. The trade-off for free access is often that your data contributes to the AI's ongoing learning.

Even within the "Private AI" category, not all systems are the same. Some offer higher levels of security and control than others:

- **Trusted Providers:** These are companies that clearly outline their privacy policies, are transparent about data usage, and allow you to opt-out of data sharing for AI training. They often comply with major data protection regulations.

- **Self-Hosted AI:** This provides the maximum control since the data never leaves your system. It requires more technical setup but offers the highest level of privacy.
- **Cloud-Based AI (with privacy features):** Even though these services may promise privacy, the data still travels over the internet to their servers. While encrypted and protected, it's important to understand that the data is still processed by a third party.

Understanding Your Data Types

In addition to categorising AI systems, it's essential to understand the types of data you're working with.

We can divide data into three simple categories based on their sensitivity:

1. **Sensitive and Confidential Data:**
    - This includes personal information (e.g., names, addresses, financial details, health records), confidential business data (e.g., unreleased product plans, financial projections, client lists, trade secrets, legal documents), and any data regulated by laws like GDPR, HIPAA, or other industry-specific regulations.
    - **Examples:** Client medical notes, unpatented invention details, employee salary information, private legal correspondence, unreleased book manuscripts.
2. **Public and Non-Sensitive Data:**
    - This is information that's already publicly

available, or data you're comfortable sharing without any risk to privacy or confidentiality. It's information that wouldn't cause harm if it became widely known.

- **Examples:** Published research papers, general knowledge queries (e.g., "What is the capital of France?"), anonymised data where all personal identifiers have been removed, or general brainstorming ideas that aren't tied to specific confidential projects.

3. **Prohibited or Illegal Content:**
    - This refers to content that is illegal, offensive, violates any platform's terms of service, or promotes harm.
    - **Examples:** Hate speech, discriminatory remarks, illegal instructions, or content that infringes on copyright. You should never input this type of content into any AI system.

How to Use the AI-Powered Data Privacy Matrix™

To decide whether it's safe to share data with an AI tool, follow these steps:

1. **Identify the AI System:**
    - Is the system Private AI or Non-Private AI?
    - Check your organisation's internal AI policies if you work for a larger company.
    - **Crucially, review the AI provider's privacy statement or terms of service.** Look for explicit language about whether your input data is used

for model training. For example, a service like ChatGPT clarifies when data is or isn't used for training (often, paid enterprise tiers offer more robust privacy guarantees).

2. **Classify the Data:**
    - Determine which of the three categories your data falls into - sensitive, public, or prohibited. Be honest and err on the side of caution. If you're unsure, treat it as sensitive.
3. **Consult the Matrix (Your Decision Rule):**
    - **If your data is Sensitive/Confidential:** Only use a **Private AI** system where you have explicit guarantees that your data will not be used for training and is securely handled. Ideally, this would be a self-hosted solution or a paid enterprise service with a strong data processing agreement.
    - **If your data is Public/Non-Sensitive:** You can generally use either **Private AI** or **Non-Private AI** systems. However, even with public data, be mindful of any terms of service that might grant the AI provider broad rights to your content.
    - **If your data is Prohibited/Illegal: Never** input this into any AI system.

Example: Applying the Framework

Let's say you want to use a free AI chatbot to summarise a business proposal that includes sensitive financial projections for a new client.

- **AI System:** Non-private (a free online chatbot with

vague or standard privacy policies that likely use your data for training).

- **Data Type:** Confidential business information (sensitive).
- **Matrix Guidance:** You should **avoid** using this chatbot for this task because the data is sensitive and the privacy of the tool is questionable. Instead, you would need to either summarise the proposal manually, or use a private AI solution that guarantees your data's confidentiality.

Additional Factors to Consider

While the matrix is a helpful guide, there are other important elements to keep in mind for robust data privacy:

- **Security Measures:** Ensure the AI system you use has strong security measures in place, such as encryption for data in transit and at rest, and robust access controls.
- **Data Retention Policies:** Understand how long your data will be stored by the AI provider. Some services delete data after a certain period, while others retain it indefinitely.
- **Share Less Data:** Only provide the minimum necessary information to the AI to get the desired output. Don't overshare. If you only need a summary of a paragraph, don't paste the entire document.
- **Anonymisation/Pseudonymisation:** When possible, remove personal identifiers or sensitive

details from the data before inputting it into an AI tool. For example, replace client names with "Client A" or "Client B."

- **Regularly Review Terms of Service:** AI providers frequently update their privacy policies and terms of service. Make it a habit to review these periodically to stay informed about any changes in how your data is handled.
- **Ethical Considerations:** Beyond legal compliance, think about the ethical implications of using certain data in AI systems. Just because something is legally permissible doesn't always make it ethically sound. Consider the potential impact on individuals or groups.
- **Employee Training:** If you have a team, ensure everyone understands these privacy guidelines and the importance of responsible AI use.

The AI-Powered Data Privacy Matrix™ gives you a structured way to protect your sensitive data when using AI systems.

By categorising both AI systems and data types, you can make informed decisions about how and when to share data, staying compliant, ethical, and secure.

Mastering data privacy in the age of AI helps you avoid risks, build trust, and maintain your professional integrity & reputation.

Key Takeaways:

- Data privacy is crucial for legal compliance, financial security, and maintaining trust.

- **Private AI** systems do not use your data for training; **Non-Private AI** systems may.
- Categorise your data as **Sensitive/Confidential**, **Public/Non-Sensitive**, or **Prohibited/Illegal**.
- Use the **AI-Powered Data Privacy Matrix**™ to decide what data to input into which AI system.
- Always prioritise **Private AI** for sensitive data.
- Fact-check privacy policies and consider security, data retention, and anonymisation.

Next Steps

Take a moment to review the privacy policies of the AI tools you currently use most often (e.g., ChatGPT, Claude, Gemini). Can you find clear statements about whether your input data is used for training? If not, consider if you're comfortable using them for sensitive information. If you are using them for sensitive information, consider upgrading to a paid tier or exploring alternative private AI solutions.

Chapter 9

Beyond Chatbots

Expanding Your AI Toolkit

Chatbots are powerful, but AI offers much more. A diverse set of AI tools can boost your creativity and make your work easier. This chapter looks at user-friendly AI tools that go beyond just chatbots.

Visuals That Pop: AI for Design & Graphics

You do not need to be a professional designer to create great visuals. AI makes design accessible to everyone.

Some popular AI design tools include:

- **Midjourney:** A leading image generation tool that creates unique artwork from text. You type what you want to see, and Midjourney generates the image.
- **ChatGPT**: ChatGPT itself now has an amazing image creator and editor inbuilt.
- **Canva:** An easy web-based platform with templates, images, and fonts. Its AI features help with colour palettes, design ideas, and creating presentations or social media graphics quickly.

These tools let you create all sorts of visual content, including:

- **Logos:** Design professional logos for your business, website, or project, even without drawing skills.

- **Presentations:** Create engaging presentations with AI-chosen colours, fonts, layouts, and image suggestions.
- **Social Media Graphics:** Design eye-catching graphics that stand out in social media feeds.
- **Artwork:** Create amazing artwork from your imagination.

Keep in mind that while these AI tools are powerful, great design still requires your creative vision and aesthetic sense.

Writing That Flows: AI for Content Creation

AI can be your writing partner, whether you write a lot or just struggle with simple emails.

Commonly used AI writing assistants include:

- **Grammarly:** A powerful spellchecker that corrects grammar and spelling errors. It also suggests better wording and improves clarity.
- **QuillBot:** Offers features similar to Grammarly. It also includes paraphrasing, plagiarism checks, and tone adjustments.

These tools help you:

- **Improve Your Writing:** Become a better writer by learning about grammar, style, and tone, with personalised feedback.
- **Save Time on Editing:** Catch mistakes you might miss. They can also rewrite sentences or paragraphs for stronger, more concise writing.

- **Repurpose Content:** Quickly paraphrase and reformat content. This works for blog posts to social media, or video scripts to articles.

Boosting Productivity: AI for Efficiency

AI can help you work smarter and faster in many areas of your life.

Some great AI productivity tools include:

- **Otter.ai**: Records and transcribes meetings, interviews, or lectures in real-time, generating searchable notes and summaries. Ideal for capturing action items without manual notetaking, and integrates with Zoom/Teams.
- **Motion**: Acts as an AI project manager, auto-scheduling tasks, meetings, and deadlines based on priorities, work patterns, and team availability. Reduces manual calendar-blocking and prevents overbooking.
- **Reclaim.ai**: Defends focus time by auto-rescheduling tasks around meetings and blocking "busy" slots for deep work. Syncs with Google Calendar to eliminate scheduling conflicts and protect routines like workouts or breaks.
- **Notion AI**: Turns your workspace into a smart assistant, summarising documents, drafting content, and answering questions using your stored data. Cuts research time and streamlines knowledge management.
- **Grammarly**: Enhances writing clarity and tone in real-time across emails, docs, and apps.

Beyond grammar checks, it suggests conciseness improvements and brand-voice consistency.

- **Fireflies.ai**: Joins calls to transcribe discussions, extract action items, and analyse speaker sentiment. Useful for creating shareable recaps and tracking decisions across meetings.
- **Clockwise**: Optimizes team calendars by bundling meetings, resolving conflicts, and protecting focus blocks. Integrates with Slack to propose ideal times across time zones.

There are many other AI tools that help boost productivity, assisting with project management, time tracking, task organisation, and automating repetitive workflows.

Exercise

Ready to explore beyond chatbots? Choose an AI tool from this chapter that interests you. Sign up for a free trial or download the app to see what it can do. You will be amazed at how AI can enhance your design, writing, and overall efficiency.

Chapter 10

Advanced Prompting Strategies and Templates

Your AI results feel generic. The outputs don't match your needs. Basic prompts aren't cutting it anymore.

This chapter shows you three simple ways to get better results from AI. No complex theory - just practical techniques you can use today.

The Problem with Basic Prompts

Most people write prompts like this: "Write a social media post about my service."

The AI gives you something generic that sounds like everyone else's content. Why? Because you haven't given it enough information to do better.

Here's the fix: treat AI like a new assistant on their first day. They're smart but know nothing about your business. The more context you give, the better they perform.

Technique 1: Give AI a Role

Start your prompts by telling AI who to be. This instantly improves the tone and relevance.

Basic: "Write an email to a client"

Better: "Act as a friendly business consultant. Write an email to a client"

Best: "You're a business consultant who values clear communication and building relationships. Write a warm but professional email to a client"

Try it yourself. Pick any task and add "Act as a..." to the beginning. Watch how the output changes.

Technique 2: Use the Before-After Method

Show AI exactly what you want by giving one example.

Here's the structure:

1. Show what you've done before
2. Ask for something similar

Example:"Here's an email I sent last week:'Hi Sarah, Thanks for our chat yesterday. I've attached the proposal we discussed. Looking forward to your thoughts. Best, John'

Write a similar email to Tom about the contract we discussed."

The AI learns your style from that one example. Much easier than trying to explain your tone.

Technique 3: Break Big Tasks into Steps

Instead of asking AI to do everything at once, break it down. Like eating a meal one bite at a time.

Too big: "Create a marketing plan for my new service"

Better - Step 1: "List 5 problems my accounting service solves for small businesses"

Step 2: "Take problem #1 and write a LinkedIn post about it"

Step 3: "Suggest 3 images that could go with this post"

Each step is simple. But together, they build something useful.

Your Power Template

Here's one template that combines all three techniques. Copy it, fill in the blanks, and watch your results improve:

```
You are a [your role/profession].You help [your target audience] with [what you do].Your style is [2-3 words describing your approach].Write a [type of content] about [topic].Make it [length].Focus on [main point or benefit].End with [call to action].
```

Real example filled in:

```
You are a career coach.You help mid-career professionals with job transitions.Your style is encouraging, practical, and honest.Write a LinkedIn post about dealing with job rejection.Make it
```

100-150 words.Focus on how rejection is redirection to better opportunities.End with asking readers to share their own comeback stories.

Common Mistakes to Avoid

1. **Making prompts too long:** If your prompt is more than a paragraph, simplify it.
2. **Using vague words:** Replace "good" or "nice" with specific descriptions like "professional" or "conversational".
3. **Asking for too much at once:** One task per prompt. You can always ask follow-up questions.

Next Steps

1. Pick three tasks you do regularly
2. Write prompts for them using the template above
3. Save the ones that work
4. Reuse them next week

That's it. No complex frameworks. No jargon. Just three techniques that make AI work better for your business.

Start with giving AI a role. Master that first. The rest will follow naturally.

Chapter 11

AI in Action

Real-World Use Cases

Theory is useful. Examples are better.

This chapter shows AI at work across industries - from healthcare to education, marketing to finance. You'll see specific ways businesses like yours use AI to solve real problems.

These aren't hypothetical scenarios. They're happening now, and they'll spark ideas for your own work.

AI in the Workplace: Boosting Business

AI is rapidly making its way into every type of workplace, from large corporations to independent businesses like yours. It's helping organisations become more efficient, productive, and competitive by automating tasks, providing insights, and enhancing decision-making.

Examples:

- **Customer Service:** AI-powered chatbots and virtual assistants are now common on many websites and phone lines, providing instant support to customers, answering frequently asked questions, and even resolving basic issues. This frees up human agents to handle more complex or sensitive inquiries.
- **Marketing and Sales:** AI is used to analyse vast

amounts of customer data, predict consumer behaviour, and personalise marketing campaigns. This helps businesses reach the right audience with the right message at the right time, leading to more effective advertising and higher conversion rates. AI can also help salespeople identify potential leads and optimise their outreach strategies.

- **Human Resources:** AI can automate repetitive HR tasks like recruiting, screening resumes, scheduling interviews, and onboarding new employees. This frees up HR professionals to focus on more strategic initiatives, such as talent development, employee engagement, and fostering a positive company culture.
- **Financial Services:** AI is used for fraud detection, risk assessment, algorithmic trading, and personalised financial advice. It can analyse market trends faster than humans, helping institutions make more informed investment decisions.
- **Manufacturing and Logistics:** AI optimises supply chains, predicts equipment failures, and manages inventory, leading to more efficient production and delivery processes. Robots powered by AI are also used for assembly and quality control.
- **Content Creation and Curation:** Beyond what we discussed in earlier chapters, businesses use AI to generate reports, summarise market research, draft internal communications, and even curate relevant news feeds for employees.

AI in Healthcare: Saving Lives and Improving Care

AI is revolutionising the healthcare industry, helping doctors diagnose diseases more accurately, personalise treatment plans, and improve patient outcomes. Its ability to process and analyse massive datasets is particularly impactful in this field.

Examples:

- **Medical Imaging Analysis:** AI-powered tools can analyse medical images like X-rays, MRIs, and CT scans with incredible speed and accuracy, helping doctors identify abnormalities, detect early signs of diseases (like cancer), and make more precise diagnoses.

- **Drug Discovery and Development:** AI is used to analyse vast amounts of data about diseases, biological compounds, and drug interactions. This accelerates the process of discovering new drugs and developing more effective treatments, significantly reducing the time and cost involved.

- **Personalised Medicine:** AI can help doctors create highly personalised treatment plans based on a patient's unique genetic makeup, medical history, lifestyle, and response to previous treatments. This leads to more effective and tailored care.

- **Predictive Analytics:** AI can predict disease outbreaks, identify patients at high risk of certain conditions, and even forecast hospital bed availability, allowing healthcare systems to prepare and allocate resources more effectively.

- **Robotics in Surgery:** AI-powered robots assist surgeons with precision tasks, leading to less invasive procedures and faster patient recovery times.

AI in Education: Tailored Learning for Everyone

AI is transforming education, helping teachers personalise instruction, create more engaging learning experiences, and provide students with customised support. It's about making learning more effective and accessible.

Examples:

- **Personalised Learning Platforms:** AI-powered platforms can track student progress, identify areas where they struggle, and adapt lessons to meet their individual needs. This provides a truly personalised learning experience, ensuring no student is left behind or held back.

- **Automated Grading and Feedback:** AI can help teachers grade assignments more efficiently, especially for objective questions or essays. This frees up their time to provide more individualised feedback, focus on complex grading, and engage in direct teaching.

- **Intelligent Tutoring Systems:** AI-powered tutors can provide students with customised support, explaining concepts in different ways, offering practice problems, and guiding them through challenging material.

- **Content Curation:** AI can help educators find and curate relevant learning materials, videos, and articles tailored to specific topics or student needs.

- **Administrative Tasks:** AI can assist with scheduling, managing student records, and other administrative burdens, allowing educators to focus more on teaching.

AI in Everyday Life: Making Things Easier

AI is becoming increasingly integrated into our everyday lives, often working silently in the background to make things easier, more efficient, and more convenient. You might not even realise you're using it!

Examples:

- **Virtual Assistants:** AI-powered virtual assistants like Siri, Alexa, and Google Assistant are now commonplace. They help us with tasks like setting reminders, playing music, answering questions, controlling smart home devices, and searching the web using voice commands.

- **Navigation and Transportation:** AI-powered navigation apps like Google Maps and Waze help us find our way around, avoid traffic jams, and discover new places. AI is also crucial for the development of self-driving cars, aiming to make roads safer and more efficient.

- **Translation Services:** AI-powered translation tools like Google Translate can help us communicate with people who speak different languages, breaking down barriers in travel and global business. Real-time translation in conversations is becoming increasingly sophisticated.

- **Shopping and Recommendations:** AI-powered recommendation engines on platforms like Amazon, Netflix, and Spotify analyse our preferences and past behaviour to suggest products, movies, or music we might like. This personalises our online experiences.

- **Smart Home Devices:** AI enables smart thermostats to learn our preferences, smart lighting to adjust based on time of day, and security cameras to detect unusual activity.

- **Spam Filters and Cybersecurity:** AI plays a vital role in filtering out spam emails and detecting malicious software or cyber threats, protecting our digital lives.

The Future of AI: Continuous Innovation

The future of AI is full of exciting possibilities. As AI technology continues to advance, we can expect to see even more innovative applications that will transform how we work, learn, and live. The examples above are just a snapshot of what's already happening. The pace of innovation is accelerating, and AI will continue to integrate more deeply into every aspect of our lives, creating new opportunities and challenges. Staying informed and adaptable will be key.

Key Takeaways:

- AI is actively transforming industries and daily life, moving beyond theoretical concepts.

- In the **workplace**, AI boosts efficiency in customer service, marketing, HR, finance, and manufacturing.

- In **healthcare**, AI improves diagnosis, drug discovery, personalised medicine, and predictive analytics.

- In **education**, AI enables personalised learning, automated grading, and intelligent tutoring.

- In **everyday life**, AI powers virtual assistants, navigation, translation, and personalised recommendations.
- The future promises continuous innovation and deeper integration of AI into all aspects of society.

Next Steps

Choose one of the real-world AI use cases discussed in this chapter that you find most interesting or relevant to your own life. Spend 15-20 minutes researching a specific company or product that is using AI in that area. How are they applying AI? What problems are they solving? This will give you a concrete understanding of AI's impact and inspire you with new possibilities.

Chapter 12

Putting It All Together

Knowledge without application stays theoretical. Let's build something real.

This chapter walks through creating a content marketing strategy using everything we've covered.

You'll see how different AI tools work together, guided by smart prompting, to produce actual business results.

We won't build a year's worth of content, but we will create a strong foundation you can expand.

Practical AI Project: Kickstarting a Content Marketing Strategy

Let's imagine you're an independent professional - perhaps a business coach specialising in helping small businesses improve their productivity - you can easily adapt this to your own field.

You want to create a series of blog posts and social media updates to establish your expertise and generate leads.

Here's how we'll approach this, using AI at various stages:

Phase 1: Brainstorming & Strategy with AI Chatbots

First, we need ideas and a basic strategy. We'll use an AI chatbot like ChatGPT or Claude, using the prompting techniques you learned.

Step 1: Defining Your Niche & Audience

Prompt using GOAL framework:

- **Goal:** Refine my understanding of my target audience for content marketing
- **Output:** A list of 3-5 key pain points and 3-5 content aspirations for my ideal client
- **Additional Context:** "I am a business coach specialising in productivity for small business owners (1-10 employees). They are often overwhelmed, struggle with time management, and want practical, actionable advice to grow their business without burning out. My content should be encouraging and solution-oriented."
- **Look:** Review the AI's suggestions. Do they resonate? Refine if needed.

Step 2: Generating Core Content Themes

Based on the audience insights, let's brainstorm some core themes.

Prompt: "Act as a content strategist. Based on the small business owner pain points of [insert AI-generated or your own pain points], suggest 3-4 pillar content themes that would be highly relevant. For each theme, suggest 2-3 specific blog post titles that would appeal to this audience and offer practical solutions."

Example AI output might include themes like "Time Management Hacks," "Delegation Strategies," "Productivity Tool Reviews," "Mindset for Success."

Step 3: Keyword Research Ideas

While dedicated SEO tools are best, AI can give us a starting point.

Prompt: "For the blog post title '[Chosen Blog Post Title, e.g., '5 Time-Saving Tools Every Small Business Owner Needs']', suggest 5-7 relevant keywords or search phrases that potential readers might use on Google."

Phase 2: Content Creation & Refinement

Now we have ideas, let's draft some content.

Step 4: Outlining a Blog Post

Choose one of your blog post titles.

Prompt (using previous output): "Using the blog post title '[Chosen Blog Post Title]' and the keywords '[Keywords from Step 3]', create a detailed outline for a 1000-word blog post. Include an introduction, 3-5 main sections with sub-points, and a conclusion with a call to action (e.g., 'book a free consultation')."

Step 5: Drafting Content Sections

Don't start by asking AI to write the whole post at once. Work section by section for better control and quality.

Prompt for introduction: "Write the introduction for the blog post based on the outline above. Make it highly engaging and clearly state what the reader will learn. Target a friendly but professional tone."

Then, for each main section: "Now, write the section titled '[Section Title from Outline]' expanding on these sub-points: [Sub-points]. Provide practical examples where possible."

Important: Human-In-The-Loop always. AI drafts are a starting point, not the end point. You, as the subject expert, need to review, edit, add your unique insights, anecdotes, and ensure factual accuracy. When you are more experienced using AI you'll be more comfortable having the AI write an entire draft all at once, but you still need to review everything it created.

Step 6: Refining with AI Writing Assistants

Once you have a first draft, you could use a tool like Grammarly or QuillBot to check for:

- Grammar and spelling errors
- Clarity and conciseness
- Tone adjustments
- Paraphrasing sections that might sound too generic

Phase 3: Visual Content Creation

Content needs visuals to grab attention.

Step 7: Creating Graphics

Let's use an AI design tool like Canva.

Process:

1. Go to Canva.com
2. Search for a template (e.g., "blog header" or "LinkedIn post")
3. Use Canva's AI features like "Magic Write" for headline ideas
4. For AI image generation, try a prompt like: "Create a professional flat design illustration for a blog post about productivity tools for small businesses. Bright, optimistic colours. Include icons representing tools like calendars, checklists, and collaboration."
5. Add your blog post title or a catchy phrase to the design

Ensure the design aligns with your branding and the image is relevant and high quality.

Phase 4: Content Promotion & Scheduling

Creating content is only half the battle - you need to promote it.

Step 8: Drafting Social Media Updates

Take your blog post and ask an AI chatbot to help repurpose it.

Prompt: "Based on the blog post titled '[Your Blog Post Title]' and its key sections [briefly list 2-3 key takeaways from your post], draft three distinct social media updates:

1. A LinkedIn post (approx. 100 words, professional tone, ask an engaging question)

2. A Twitter/X thread (3-4 tweets, concise, use relevant hashtags)
3. An Instagram caption (focus on a key visual aspect or a relatable problem, use emojis)"

Edit these for natural language and add your personality. Ensure any links to your blog post are correct.

Step 9: Planning a Content Schedule

Prompt: "I plan to publish one new blog post per week and promote it on LinkedIn, Twitter/X, and Instagram. Suggest a simple weekly content promotion schedule. For example, on which days should I post the initial announcement, and on which days could I post follow-up reminders or related snippets?"

This gives you a framework to then manually schedule using your preferred tools.

Phase 5: Data Privacy & Ethical Considerations

Throughout this entire project, keep in mind what we learned about data privacy and responsible AI:

Sensitive Information: Are you inputting any confidential client data or unreleased business strategies into non-private AI tools? For general brainstorming and public-facing content drafts, it's usually fine, but be cautious.

Originality: AI-generated text can sometimes be generic or inadvertently similar to existing content. Always add your unique perspective and consider using a plagiarism checker if you're relying heavily on AI drafts.

Transparency: Consider if and how you'll disclose AI assistance in your content. For your own internal strategy and drafts, it's your choice. For client-facing work, transparency is often best.

Your AI-Augmented Workflow

This project demonstrates a simplified workflow. In reality, you'd iterate, go deeper into each step, and use more specialised tools. But you can see the potential:

- **AI as brainstormer** - helping you overcome the blank page
- **AI as drafter** - giving you a solid first pass, saving hours
- **AI as editor** - polishing your language
- **AI as designer** - helping create appealing visuals
- **AI as repurposer** - maximising the reach of your core content

By integrating these AI tools and techniques, guided by your expertise and critical oversight, you can build a robust content marketing approach without needing a large team or enormous budget.

Key Takeaways

- AI can assist in nearly every stage of content marketing, from ideation to promotion
- Combining different AI tools creates a powerful, integrated workflow
- Effective prompting is crucial for getting

high-quality outputs

- Human oversight, editing, and expertise remain essential for quality, accuracy, and authenticity
- Always consider data privacy and ethical implications when using AI

Next Steps

Your turn. Don't just read about it - try it.

1. **Choose a small piece of content you'd like to create for your own business** (e.g., one blog post idea, a series of 3 social media posts on a specific topic)
2. **Work through at least 3-4 steps from our project outline above** using the AI tools you've set up (e.g., brainstorm with a chatbot, draft an outline, create a simple visual with Canva)
3. **Reflect:** How did AI help? Where did you still need to provide significant input? What was easier or faster than doing it entirely manually?

This hands-on experience, even on a small scale, will be the most valuable way to solidify your learning and see how AI can truly become your partner in building your authority.

Chapter 13

AI Workflows for Different Industries

Generic AI advice rarely fits specific businesses. What works for a consultant differs from what a coach needs.

This chapter provides targeted workflows for your industry. You'll find practical examples, time-saving templates, and ways to adapt AI to your unique challenges.

Skip to your section for immediate value, then read the others for fresh ideas.

AI for Consultants

Consultants rely on efficiency, data analysis, and clear communication. AI can become a valuable partner in each of these areas, allowing you to deliver greater value to clients more quickly.

Your Quick Win: AI for Rapid Market Research

One of the more time-consuming initial tasks for a consultant involves market research for a new client or project. AI can significantly reduce this effort.

Quick Win Prompt Example:

Act as a market research analyst specialising in [Client's Industry, e.g., renewable energy]. Your task is to identify key trends, emerging challenges, and major competitors for a new startup focused on [Client's Specific Niche, e.g., smart home battery solutions]. Provide your findings in a concise bullet-point summary, including relevant statistics if available. The tone should be analytical and objective.

This prompt provides a starting point for comprehensive market research, saving hours of manual searching.

How can AI assist with market research for new clients?

AI can swiftly sift through vast amounts of data - industry reports, news articles, academic papers, and social media trends - to identify patterns and insights that would take a human weeks to uncover. Tools like ChatGPT (with browsing capabilities) or specialised AI research platforms can:

- **Identify Key Trends:** Ask AI to summarise the top 5 emerging trends in a specific industry over the last 12-24 months.
- **Analyse Competitors:** Provide AI with a list of competitors and ask for a SWOT analysis or a comparison of their service offerings.
- **Spot Market Gaps:** Describe a target market and ask AI to identify underserved needs or potential niches.

Case Study: Rachel, a management consultant, used AI to research the impact of supply chain disruptions on the automotive industry for a new client pitch. Within 30 minutes, AI provided a summary of recent reports, key affected regions, and potential mitigation strategies, allowing Rachel to tailor her proposal with highly relevant, up-to-date information. This efficiency gain meant she could focus more on strategic recommendations rather than data collection.

What AI tools are best for drafting proposals and reports?

Generative AI models are excellent for structuring and drafting professional documents.

- **ChatGPT/Claude/Gemini:** Ideal for generating initial drafts, outlines, executive summaries, and specific sections of proposals or reports. You can prompt them with project details, client requirements, and desired outcomes.
- **Grammarly/QuillBot:** Beyond grammar checks, these tools can refine your language, adjust tone, and paraphrase sections for clarity and impact, ensuring your proposals are polished and persuasive.

How can AI streamline client communication and follow-ups?

Maintaining consistent, professional client communication is crucial.

AI can help automate repetitive aspects.

- **Email Drafting:** Use AI to draft polite follow-up emails, meeting recaps, or responses to common client queries. Give it your key points and let AI handle the phrasing, but always review and adjust to maintain your authentic voice.
- **Meeting Summaries:** Combine voice AI tools (like Otter.ai for transcription) with text AI (like

ChatGPT for summarisation) to quickly create meeting minutes and action item lists from audio recordings.

- **Personalised Updates:** With structured data (e.g., client progress in a CRM), AI can help draft personalised update emails, freeing your time for more impactful client engagement.

AI for Coaches and Trainers

Coaches and trainers focus on individual growth and effective knowledge transfer.

AI offers unique opportunities to personalise learning, streamline administrative tasks, and enhance content delivery.

Your Quick Win: AI for Personalised Practice Prompts

For coaches, providing tailored exercises or reflection prompts is key. AI can generate these instantly.

Quick Win Prompt Example:

"Act as an experienced executive coach. My client is a mid-career professional struggling with time management and delegation. Generate 3 actionable reflection questions or small exercises they can do this week to improve their delegation skills. Keep the tone encouraging and concise."

This allows you to quickly create bespoke client assignments, adding immediate value to your sessions.

How can AI help personalise learning plans for clients?

Every client is unique. AI can help tailor educational content and exercises to individual needs.

- **Content Curation:** Based on a client's stated goals or challenges, AI can suggest relevant articles, videos, or exercises from a larger knowledge base.
- **Customised Explanations:** If a client struggles with a specific concept, use AI to re-explain it in different ways (e.g., "Explain [concept] as if to a complete beginner," or "Provide an analogy for [concept]").
- **Progress Tracking Prompts:** AI can generate prompts for clients to reflect on their progress, identify roadblocks, or plan next steps, making self-directed learning more effective.

What AI tools can assist with transcribing and summarising coaching sessions?

Insights from coaching sessions are invaluable, but manual note-taking can be distracting.

- **Otter.ai/Whisper:** These tools excel at accurately transcribing spoken dialogue. You can record sessions (with client consent) and get a full text record.
- **ChatGPT/Claude (with transcript input):** Once you have a transcript, feed it into a large language model and prompt for summaries, key themes, action items, or even identifying recurring patterns in client challenges. This transforms raw data into actionable insights.

How can AI support content creation for workshops and courses?

Developing engaging workshop materials or online courses is a significant time investment. AI can accelerate this.

- **Brainstorming Content:** Prompt AI for module ideas, lesson plans, or specific activities related to your course topic.
- **Drafting Handouts/Slides:** Generate outlines, key takeaways, or even full paragraphs for your workshop handouts or presentation slides.
- **Quiz/Assessment Creation:** Ask AI to generate multiple-choice questions or short answer prompts based on your course content to test understanding.

Case Study: Alex, a fitness trainer, found creating personalised meal plans and workout routines for dozens of clients extremely time-consuming. By feeding client data (goals, allergies, preferences) into a custom AI tool, he could generate first drafts of tailored plans in minutes, allowing him to focus on client interaction and motivation. His client retention increased by 10% as a direct result of more personalised support.

AI for Freelancers and Small Business Owners

Freelancers and small business owners often manage multiple roles. AI can be a crucial assistant for automating tedious tasks, optimising marketing efforts, and enhancing customer interactions, freeing you to focus on core services and growth.

Your Quick Win: AI for Social Media Content Ideas

Generating fresh social media content consistently can be challenging. AI makes this simpler.

Quick Win Prompt Example:

Act as a social media content strategist for a freelance [Your Niche, e.g., photographer]. Brainstorm 5 engaging Instagram post ideas for this week that will attract new clients. Focus on [Specific Goal, e.g., showcasing portfolio, offering quick tips]. Include relevant hashtags.

This provides immediate, tailored content ideas, eliminating creative blocks.

How can AI automate administrative tasks for solo-entrepreneurs?

The administrative burden can be substantial for solo professionals. AI can alleviate much of this load.

- **Email Management:** Use AI to draft replies to common inquiries, sort emails, or summarise long threads.
- **Scheduling:** AI-powered scheduling tools (like Motion) can manage your calendar, find optimal meeting times, and send invitations without manual intervention.
- **Data Entry/Organisation:** For structured data, AI can help extract information from documents and populate spreadsheets, or organise client information.

What AI tools are best for generating marketing content and social media updates?

Consistent, high-quality marketing is vital for growth. AI excels at content generation.

- **ChatGPT/Claude:** Perfect for drafting blog posts, article outlines, email newsletters, website copy, and social media captions. Provide your topic, tone, and audience, and let the AI generate the initial draft.
- **Canva AI/Midjourney/DALL-E:** For visuals, these tools generate unique images, graphics, and even simple video clips from text prompts, making your marketing visually appealing without needing design skills.
- **Grammarly/QuillBot:** Refine your marketing copy for clarity, impact, and tone, ensuring your message resonates with your audience.

How can AI help with basic financial analysis or customer support?

Even without a dedicated finance or support team, AI can provide significant assistance.

- **Basic Financial Summaries:** If you have structured financial data, AI can help summarise trends, identify key metrics, or even flag anomalies (e.g., "Summarise monthly expenses and identify the top 3 spending categories").
- **Customer Service Chatbots:** For simple, repetitive customer inquiries, AI-powered chatbots can handle initial questions, freeing you to address more complex client needs. Many website builders

now offer easy chatbot integrations.

- **FAQ Generation:** Feed your existing customer questions and answers to AI, and it can help generate a comprehensive FAQ section for your website or onboarding materials.

Case Study: Jamie, a small e-commerce business owner selling handmade crafts, used to spend hours responding to repetitive customer queries and drafting product descriptions. By implementing an AI chatbot for FAQs and using AI writing tools for product descriptions, he reduced his daily administrative load by 40%, allowing him to focus on craft production and business strategy. His online reviews also improved due to faster customer service.

Key Takeaways

1. **Tailored AI Workflows:** AI offers specific, actionable solutions for various industries, including consulting, coaching, and small business.
2. **Consultants' AI Edge:** Use AI for research, proposals, and communication.
3. **Coaches' & Trainers' AI Impact:** Use AI to personalise learning and session summaries.
4. **Freelancers' & Small Business Owners' AI Boost:** Automate administrative tasks, generate compelling marketing content, and enhance customer support with AI.

Your Next Action

Identify one specific task in your industry that AI could help with. Research AI tools mentioned in this chapter or elsewhere that are designed for that task. Experiment with a free trial or a basic version to see its potential impact on your workflow.

Chapter 14

Building Your Personal AI System

Individual AI tools help. An integrated system transforms your work.

This chapter guides you through creating a cohesive AI system that enhances your existing workflow. You'll assess what you have, identify integration points, and build something that grows with your business.

Random tools create complexity. A systemised approach will be far more efficient for you.

Assessing Your Current Workflow

Building an effective personal AI system begins with understanding where AI can provide the most value. Trying to implement AI everywhere at once can lead to overwhelm and poor results. Instead, focus on your biggest pain points.

Your Quick Win: The Workflow Assessment Checklist

To identify AI integration opportunities, start with a simple workflow assessment. This quick win will highlight areas where AI can make an immediate impact.

Workflow Assessment Checklist:

- **List your 3 most time-consuming daily or weekly tasks.** Be specific (e.g., "drafting client emails," "researching market trends," "summarising meeting notes").
- **Identify 2 repetitive tasks you dread doing.** These are prime candidates for automation.
- **Pinpoint 1 "bottleneck" in your workflow.** Where does work slow down or require excessive manual effort?
- **Note any digital tools you use frequently** (e.g., email client, CRM, project management software). How might AI integrate with these?

By answering these questions, you gain clarity on where AI can offer the most significant time savings and efficiency gains for *your* unique workflow.

What are the most repetitive tasks in your daily routine?

Repetitive tasks are perfect for AI automation.

These include data entry, scheduling, drafting routine communications, content repurposing, or summarising information.

For example, if you spend an hour each day writing similar client updates, AI can draft these in minutes.

If you manually transcribe meeting notes, voice AI can do it instantly. Identifying these "low-hanging fruit" tasks provides clear starting points for AI integration.

Where do you currently experience bottlenecks or inefficiencies?

Bottlenecks are points in your workflow where progress slows or stops due to manual effort or complexity. Perhaps gathering research before a client proposal takes too long, or creating social media visuals for your new product is a major time sink. AI can act as a force multiplier at these points. For example:

- **Research Bottleneck:** Use AI to quickly summarise industry reports or competitor analyses.
- **Content Creation Bottleneck:** Use AI to generate first drafts of blog posts, social media captions, or ad copy.
- **Scheduling Bottleneck:** Implement an AI scheduling assistant to manage appointments.

What digital tools do you use regularly, and how could AI enhance them?

Consider your existing digital ecosystem. AI rarely replaces your core tools; instead, it enhances them.

- **Email Client (Outlook, Gmail):** AI tools can draft replies, summarise long threads, or even sort your inbox.
- **Project Management Software (Asana, Trello):** AI can generate task breakdowns, draft project summaries, or help brainstorm solutions to project roadblocks.
- **CRM (Salesforce, HubSpot):** AI can help draft personalised client follow-ups based on customer

data, or summarise client interaction history.

- **Design Tools (Canva, Figma):** AI can generate image ideas, create initial layouts, or remove backgrounds automatically.

Case Study: Maria, a freelance content marketer, spent hours each week creating social media content from her blog posts. By integrating an AI writing tool with her content calendar, she could now repurpose a single blog post into 10 unique social media updates (for LinkedIn, Instagram, X) in under 15 minutes, a task that previously took her two hours. This saved her over 6 hours a week, which she reinvested into client acquisition.

Designing Your AI Integration Points

Once you know *where* AI can help, the next step is designing *how*. This involves identifying specific points in your workflow where AI tools can seamlessly plug in, automating data transfer and intelligent actions. This is important because a well-designed integration makes AI feel like a natural extension of your work, not an added complication.

How can AI automate data transfer between tools?

Automation tools, often called "integrations" or "connectors," allow different apps to "talk" to each other. AI can enhance these connections by performing intelligent actions on the data as it moves.

- **Zapier/Make.com (formerly Integromat):** These platforms allow you to connect thousands of apps. You can set up "Zaps" or "Scenarios" where, for example:
    - A new email (trigger) is summarised by AI (action)

and sent to your project management tool.

  - A new meeting transcript (trigger) is analysed by AI for action items (action) and added to your task list.

- **Custom API Integrations:** For more advanced users, direct API connections can allow AI models to interact directly with your business software, automating complex data processing.

What processes can be partially or fully automated with AI?

Consider tasks that are rule-based, repetitive, or involve large datasets.

- **Content Generation (Partial/Full):** AI can draft entire articles, but you provide the final polish. Or, it can fully generate short, routine social media posts.
- **Data Analysis (Partial):** AI can summarise key trends from spreadsheets, but human interpretation is still needed for strategic insights.
- **Customer Support (Partial):** Chatbots handle FAQs, freeing human agents for complex issues.
- **Lead Qualification (Partial):** AI can score leads based on criteria, but human review confirms suitability.

Case Study: John, a solo financial advisor, used to manually extract key data points from client financial statements and input them into a spreadsheet. By using a combination of an AI data extraction tool and Zapier, he automated this process. Now, when a new statement arrives in his inbox, AI extracts the data, inputs it into his spreadsheet, and notifies him. This saves him roughly

2 hours per client, allowing him to serve more clients with less administrative overhead.

How can you set up notifications or triggers for AI-driven actions?

Notifications ensure you are aware of AI's progress or when your input is needed. Triggers initiate AI actions automatically.

- **Email Notifications:** Set up automation to email you when AI completes a task (e.g., "Your meeting summary is ready").
- **Slack/Teams Alerts:** Integrate AI tools with your communication platforms to receive real-time alerts.
- **Conditional Triggers:** Use automation platforms to trigger AI actions based on conditions (e.g., "If a new lead is added to CRM, then AI drafts a personalised welcome email").

Iterating and Optimising Your AI System

Building a personal AI system is not a one-time setup; it is an ongoing process of testing, measuring, and refining. The AI landscape evolves rapidly, and your workflows change. Continuous iteration ensures your system remains efficient and effective.

How will you measure the impact of AI on your productivity?

Measuring impact is crucial for justifying your investment in AI and identifying areas for improvement.

- **Time Tracking:** Use a time-tracking tool (e.g., Toggl, Clockify) to compare the time spent on tasks before and after AI integration.
- **Output Quality:** Establish criteria for measuring the quality of AI-generated content (e.g., relevance, conciseness, tone alignment).
- **Client/Customer Feedback:** Collect feedback on improved response times or personalised services.
- **Revenue/Profit Impact:** For business owners, track if time savings translate into more clients, services, or revenue.

Case Study: Alex, a freelance copywriter, implemented AI for drafting initial content outlines. She tracked her time for creating outlines manually versus using AI. After two weeks, she found AI reduced outline creation time by 60%, allowing her to take on two additional projects per month, directly increasing her income by 15%.

What are common challenges in AI integration, and how can you overcome them?

- **Data Privacy Concerns:** Ensure you are using AI tools that comply with data protection regulations (e.g., GDPR, HIPAA) if handling sensitive client data. Opt for enterprise-level versions where available.
- **Over-reliance on AI:** Remember AI is a tool, not a replacement for critical thinking or human oversight. Always review AI outputs for accuracy, tone, and context.
- **"Garbage In, Garbage Out":** Poorly structured prompts lead to poor results. Invest time in refining

your prompting skills.

- **Tool Overwhelm:** Resist the urge to adopt every new AI tool. Stick to tools that solve specific, identified problems in your workflow.

How can you stay updated on new AI tools and best practices for continuous improvement?

The AI landscape changes rapidly. Staying informed ensures your system remains cutting-edge.

- **Subscribe to Industry Newsletters:** Follow reputable AI news sources and technology blogs relevant to independent professionals.
- **Join Online Communities:** Engage with other professionals using AI (e.g., LinkedIn groups, specific AI tool forums).
- **Experiment Regularly:** Dedicate a small amount of time each week to trying new prompts, features, or even a new AI tool.
- **Revisit Your Workflow Assessment:** Periodically re-evaluate your workflow (e.g., quarterly) to identify new opportunities for AI integration.

Key Takeaways

1. **Assess your workflow:** Identify repetitive tasks, bottlenecks, and existing digital tools where AI can provide the most significant impact.
2. **Design integration points:** Plan how AI tools will seamlessly connect and automate actions within your existing processes, potentially using

automation platforms like Zapier.

3. **Iterate and optimise:** Continuously test, measure the impact of AI on your productivity (time, quality, revenue), and refine your system to remain efficient and competitive.

4. **Stay informed and ethical:** Be aware of data privacy, avoid over-reliance on AI, refine prompting, and stay updated on evolving AI tools and best practices.

Your Next Action

Map out one of your current daily or weekly workflows, choosing a task that consumes significant time. Identify at least two specific points within that workflow where AI could be integrated to save time or improve output. Research a specific AI tool for each integration point, or craft a detailed prompt for a general AI. Outline a simple plan for testing its impact this week, tracking the time saved and the quality improvement compared to your usual method. Be ready to adapt and refine your approach based on your findings.

Chapter 15

Strategic AI Integration

Making AI Work for Your Professional Life

You know what AI can do. You have the tools. Now what?

This chapter helps you integrate AI strategically - not everywhere, but where it matters most.

You'll identify high-impact opportunities, choose the right tools, and scale gradually.

The goal isn't to use AI for everything. It's to use it where it genuinely improves your work and life.

Finding Your High-Impact AI Opportunities

Not all tasks are created equal when it comes to AI assistance.

You want to find your "AI sweet spot" - those areas where AI can provide the most significant return on your investment of time in learning and using it.

The RATES Framework

To identify these opportunities, conduct a quick audit of your weekly tasks using this framework:

Repetitive: What tasks do you do over and over again, almost on autopilot? (e.g., drafting similar emails, data entry, scheduling, creating standard reports, formatting documents). *AI potential: High. AI excels at automating repetitive tasks.*

Annoying/Avoided: What tasks do you dread, procrastinate on, or find particularly draining, even if they are necessary? (e.g., transcribing meeting notes, initial research, proofreading long documents, updating spreadsheets). *AI potential: High. Offloading these can significantly boost your morale and productivity.*

Time-Consuming: Which tasks take up a disproportionate amount of your valuable time, even if they aren't necessarily repetitive or annoying? (e.g., in-depth research, creating detailed presentations from scratch, analysing data, writing comprehensive reports). *AI potential: Medium to High. AI can often accelerate these tasks significantly.*

Error-Prone: Are there tasks where human error can easily creep in, leading to rework or problems? (e.g., manual data transfer, complex calculations, ensuring consistent formatting across documents). *AI potential: Medium. AI can improve accuracy in rule-based tasks.*

Scalable: What tasks, if you could do more of them or do them better, would directly benefit your work or career, but you're currently limited by your own capacity? (e.g., creating more high-quality content, analysing more market data, learning new skills faster). *AI potential: High. AI can act as a force multiplier.*

Exercise

Take 15 minutes right now. List 5-10 common tasks in your work.

Rate each one using this framework. Which tasks score high on multiple factors? These are your prime candidates for AI integration.

Choosing the Right AI Tools

Once you've identified tasks, you need to find the right tools. With so many AI tools emerging, how do you choose? Use this checklist:

Purpose alignment: Does this tool directly address the task I identified? Avoid shiny object syndrome - focus on solving real problems.

Ease of use: How steep is the learning curve? For beginners, tools with intuitive interfaces and good tutorials are best.

Integration with existing workflow: Can this tool easily fit into how you already work, or will it require a major overhaul? Sometimes simpler, more focused tools are better than complex platforms if they slot in smoothly.

Quality of output: Does the AI produce results that are genuinely helpful and high quality for your specific needs? Test with small, real-world examples.

Pricing and value: Does the cost (if any) justify the time saved or value created? Start with free tiers or trials where possible.

Data privacy and security: How does this tool handle your data? Is it suitable for the type of information you'll be inputting? Consider your workplace policies on data sharing.

Developer reputation and support: Is the tool from a reputable developer? Is there good documentation, community support, or customer service if you run into issues?

The "Crawl, Walk, Run" Approach

Don't try to revolutionise your entire work routine with AI overnight. This often leads to overwhelm and frustration. Instead, adopt this approach:

Crawl (One Task, One Tool)

Pick one high-potential task from your audit. Select one promising AI tool for that task using the checklist above. Focus on learning that single tool for that single task. Get comfortable. See tangible results.

Example: Use ChatGPT to help you draft outlines for your weekly reports or presentations.

Walk (Expand Gradually)

Once you're comfortable and seeing benefits with your first tool/task, identify another related task or explore more features of the tool you're already using. Or, introduce a second, complementary tool for a different task.

Example: After mastering report outlines, use ChatGPT to help draft initial sections. Or, introduce Grammarly to polish your writing.

Run (Integrate & Automate)

As you become more proficient, look for opportunities to connect different AI tools into workflows. Explore more advanced features or even custom solutions if appropriate.

Continuously re-evaluate your audit as your skills and AI capabilities grow.

Example: Use Otter.ai to transcribe meetings, feed the transcript to ChatGPT to summarise and extract action items, then use ChatGPT to draft follow-up emails.

Overcoming Mental Blocks

It's natural to feel some hesitation or resistance when adopting new technologies, especially one as transformative as AI. Here are common mental blocks and how to address them:

"It's too complicated / I'm not techy enough"

Many AI tools are designed for beginners. Focus on user-friendly tools. Start very simply with the "crawl" phase.

"AI will take my job / make me obsolete"

Think of AI as an assistant or force multiplier. It handles routine work, freeing you to focus on strategy, creativity, relationships, and the human elements AI can't replicate. Your expertise and judgment guide the AI.

"I don't have time to learn another new thing"

The initial time investment in learning a well-chosen AI tool can save you significantly more time in the long run. Start with a task that is a major time sink. Even 15-30 minutes of focused learning per week can yield results.

"The outputs are generic / not good enough"

This often comes down to prompting skills and understanding AI's limitations. AI is a collaborator, not a magic button. Your input and refinement are key.

"My workplace doesn't allow AI tools"

Start by understanding your organisation's AI policies. Many workplaces are developing guidelines rather than blanket bans. Focus on learning with personal projects while these policies evolve, so you're ready when they do.

"Fear of the unknown / Ethical concerns"

By understanding AI and making conscious choices about tools and data, you remain in control. Focus on responsible AI use and educate yourself about the tools you're considering.

The Mindset Shift

Strategically implementing AI is more than just using tools - it's a mindset shift. It's about:

- **Continuous learning:** The AI field is always evolving. Stay curious.
- **Experimentation:** Be willing to try new tools and techniques (starting small).
- **Valuing your time:** Actively look for ways AI can free you from low-value tasks.
- **Focusing on your unique human strengths:** Let AI handle what it does best, so you can excel at what you do best - critical thinking, creativity, empathy, and building genuine connections.

By strategically integrating AI, you're not replacing your skills - you're amplifying them. You're building a more efficient, effective, and ultimately more satisfying professional life.

Key Takeaways

- Strategically integrate AI by first identifying high-impact opportunities using the RATES audit (Repetitive, Annoying, Time-Consuming, Error-Prone, Scalable)
- Evaluate potential AI tools using purpose alignment, ease of use, integration, quality, price, privacy, and reputation
- Adopt a "Crawl, Walk, Run" approach to start small, build confidence, and scale AI usage gradually
- Acknowledge and address common mental blocks regarding AI complexity, job displacement, time investment, output quality, and workplace policies
- Embrace a mindset of continuous learning and experimentation

Next Steps

1. **Perform your RATES audit** for your work tasks this week. Identify your top 1-2 AI opportunities.
2. For one of those tasks, research 1-2 potential AI tools using the checklist above.
3. Commit to the "Crawl" phase: Spend 30-60 minutes in the next week learning and applying one chosen tool to that one task.

4. **Reflect:** What mental blocks, if any, did you notice in yourself as you considered this? How can you reframe them?

This strategic approach will ensure that AI becomes a true asset to your professional life, tailored to your specific needs and goals.

Chapter 16

AI Glossary

Key Terms for Beginners

This glossary explains AI terms in plain English. Each definition focuses on what you need to know to use AI tools effectively.

A

AI (Artificial Intelligence): Computer programs that perform tasks requiring human intelligence - like learning, problem-solving, and making decisions. When Netflix suggests films you might like, that's AI at work.

AI Agent: A program that acts independently to achieve goals. Unlike chatbots that only respond to questions, agents can complete multi-step tasks on their own - like booking meetings or managing calendars.

AI Chatbot: A program you can talk to using text, or sometimes voice. It uses AI to understand your questions and give helpful, human-like responses. ChatGPT, Claude, and Gemini are examples.

Algorithm: Step-by-step instructions a computer follows to solve problems. Like a recipe, but for computers.

B

Bias: When AI shows unfairness toward certain groups or ideas. This happens when training data reflects existing prejudices. An AI trained only on images of men in leadership roles might struggle to recognise women in similar positions.

Brainstorming: Coming up with new ideas. AI makes an excellent brainstorming partner by suggesting options you might not consider.

C

ChatGPT: A popular AI chatbot by OpenAI. Known for understanding and generating human-like text for writing, coding, and answering questions.

Claude: An AI chatbot by Anthropic. Good at handling longer conversations and analytical tasks.

Cloud Computing: Accessing computer programs and storing data over the Internet, rather than directly on your personal device. Most AI tools you use operate in the cloud.

Context: Background information that helps AI understand your request. Without enough context, AI might misunderstand what you need.

Context Window: How much text an AI can "remember" during a conversation. Like short-term memory - if conversations get too long, earlier parts might be forgotten.

Custom GPT: A personalised AI assistant you can create with specific instructions and knowledge for your business or task.

D

Data: Information (like text, images, or numbers) that computers can process. AI learns from large amounts of this data to identify patterns and make predictions. The quality and diversity of this data heavily influence AI's performance and potential for bias.

Data Privacy: Protecting personal information from unauthorised collection or sharing. Critical when using AI tools with sensitive information.

F

Fact-Checking: Verifying AI-generated information for accuracy. Essential because AI can sometimes "hallucinate" or provide outdated information.

Few-Shot Learning: Teaching AI by showing 2-5 examples of what you want. The AI learns from these examples and applies that understanding to new tasks.

Fine-tuning: Training a general AI model on specific data to make it better at particular tasks or adapt it to your style.

G

Generative AI: AI that creates new, original content – like text, images, music, code, or video. ChatGPT (for text) and Midjourney (for images) are examples.

GOAL Framework: A simple method for writing effective AI prompts: Goal (what you want), Output (format needed), Additional Context (background info), Look at the Output (review and refine).

H

Hallucination: When AI generates false information but presents it as true. A common challenge requiring vigilance.

L

Large Language Model (LLM): AI trained on massive amounts of text to understand and generate language. ChatGPT, Claude, and Gemini are LLMs.

M

Machine Learning (ML): How computers learn from data without explicit programming. They identify patterns and use them to make decisions.

N

Natural Language: How humans naturally speak and write. AI increasingly understands natural language, making interactions more intuitive.

O

Output: What AI produces in response to your prompt.

P

Prompt: The instruction or question you give AI. Your starting point for any AI interaction.

Prompt Chaining: Using the output from one prompt as input for the next, automating multi-step tasks.

Prompt Engineering: The skill of crafting effective prompts to guide AI to produce the best, most accurate, and most useful results.

Prompt Template: A reusable prompt with placeholders for consistent results on similar tasks.

R

RATES Framework: A method to identify tasks where AI helps most: Repetitive, Annoying, Time-Consuming, Error-Prone, or Scalable tasks.

Repetitive Task: Tasks done the same way repeatedly. AI excels at automating these.

Role: Telling AI what function to perform when responding. Helps focus the AI's knowledge appropriately.

S

Shadow AI: Using AI tools at work without company approval. Can create security risks.

Structured Prompting: Giving AI specific, detailed instructions using frameworks or templates for precise outputs.

Summarising: Condensing long text into key points. AI excels at this task.

T

Temperature (AI): A setting in some AI models that controls the randomness of its output. Higher temperature leads to more creative, diverse, and sometimes unexpected or less factual responses. Lower temperature results in more focused, predictable, and often more factual responses.

Token: A unit of text AI uses - could be a word, part of a word, or punctuation. Context windows are measured in tokens.

Training Data: Information used to teach AI models. Quality and diversity of this data affects AI capabilities and biases.

V

Virtual Assistant: An AI program designed to help with tasks like answering questions, scheduling, finding information, or controlling smart devices. Siri and Alexa are common examples, and many AI chatbots also function as virtual assistants.

W

Workflow: Steps to complete a task. AI can automate parts of workflows for efficiency.

Z

Zero-Shot Learning: Asking AI to perform tasks without examples, relying on its general knowledge.

This glossary covers the essential terms you'll encounter when using AI tools. Focus on understanding these core concepts first - you can explore more specialised terminology as you gain experience.

What's Next? Stay Curious.

AI is changing fast, and that won't slow down.

The skills you've learned here are solid. They'll serve you well. But they're a starting point, not the finish line.

New tools emerge every month. Some disappear, others improve overnight. That's why staying curious, thoughtful, and adaptable is the key to long-term success with AI. The good news is you now have the foundation to evaluate these changes and decide what's worth your time.

Ready to Go Further?

We've covered the basics in this guide - prompting, verification, daily integration. But there's more to consider if you're thinking strategically about AI, especially around risk and implementation, and how to apply it across your team or business. I've created a free resource to help you take the next step with confidence:

Get the Complete AI Toolkit: Opportunity, Risk & Roadmap to AI Success

This in-depth series of three whitepapers goes beyond daily tools and tips. It's built from real-world experience and designed to help you:

- **Identify high-impact opportunities** for AI in your

business

- **Mitigate risks** like bias, data privacy, and over-reliance
- **Follow a structured roadmap** to roll out AI with clarity and purpose

You can download the full toolkit – no email required – at **humanspark.ai/toolkit**

Let's Keep the Conversation Going

I'd love to hear your thoughts, ideas, or questions on using AI – what's working for you, and where you're still figuring things out.

Drop me a note any time: **alastair@humanspark.ai** – I read and reply to every message personally.

About the Author

Alastair McDermott shows business leaders and employees how to work smarter and faster with AI - then scale those wins across your team and organisation.

Turn AI into real productivity gains for you and your team. Use AI to automate repetitive tasks, increase productivity, and drive innovation, all while keeping a Human First approach. This enables your team to achieve more, focus on strategic initiatives, and make your company a more enjoyable place to work.

He is a consultant, speaker and AI coach who hosts *The AI-Powered Business Leader podcast*. He works directly with business leaders in Co-Builder™ sessions to deliver a custom AI solution for your most pressing task, live in 90 minutes.

Expert Authority Builder Series:

- *An Absolute Beginner's Guide to Using AI* (2024 – updated 2025) - Learn how to use AI tools to boost your productivity and get more done, with no technical background required.
- *The AI-Powered Thought Leader* (2024 – updated 2025) - How to harness AI to expand your influence, boost productivity, and build a stronger personal brand.
- *Quick-Win Content* (2023) - A practical guide to

creating engaging content that resonates with clients and generates leads.

- *Efficient Content Creation* (2023) - Learn how to create high-quality content consistently, even with a busy schedule.
- *Your Podcast Launch Workbook* (2022) - Everything you need to plan, record, and launch a successful business podcast.

Other Books and Guides:

- *33 Ways Not to Screw Up Your Business Podcast* (2022) - Avoid common podcasting mistakes and create a show that gets results.
- *How to Sound & Look Good on Zoom & Podcasts* (2022) - Essential tips and recommendations for presenting yourself professionally online.
- *Running a Website with WordPress* (2015) - A comprehensive guide to building and managing a website using WordPress.

Find all of Alastair's books at **humanspark.ai/allbooks**

Alastair lives on the beautiful west coast of Ireland. He is addicted to sports of all kinds, and he reads more science fiction and fantasy than most would consider healthy.

Printed in Dunstable, United Kingdom

68558729R00080